Kaleidoscope Patterns

Adult Coloring Book

This book is dedicated to Janet, Jackie, and Marilyn. Three lovely ladies that love patterns just as much as I do!

Enjoy!

by:

Jules Baker

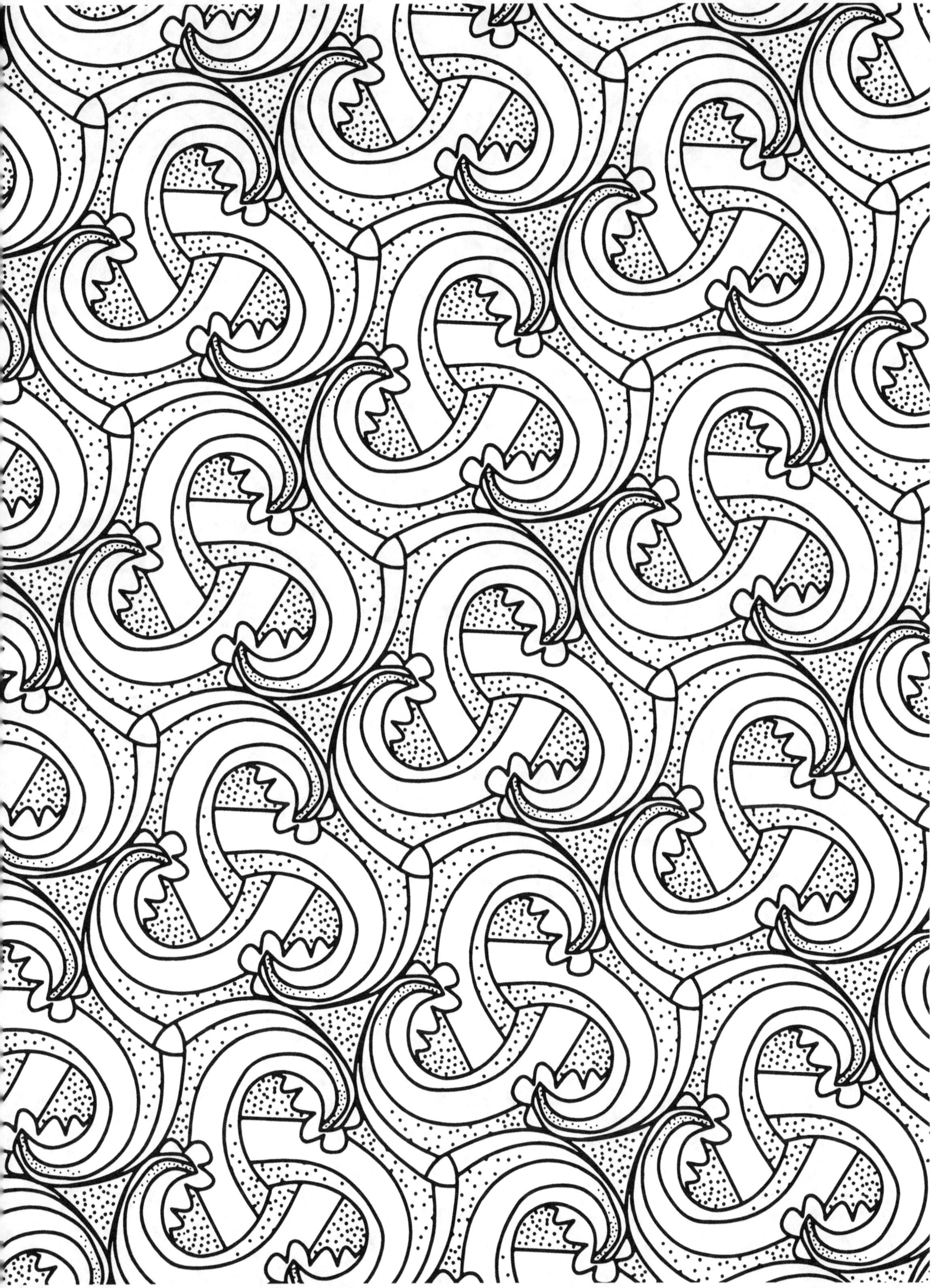

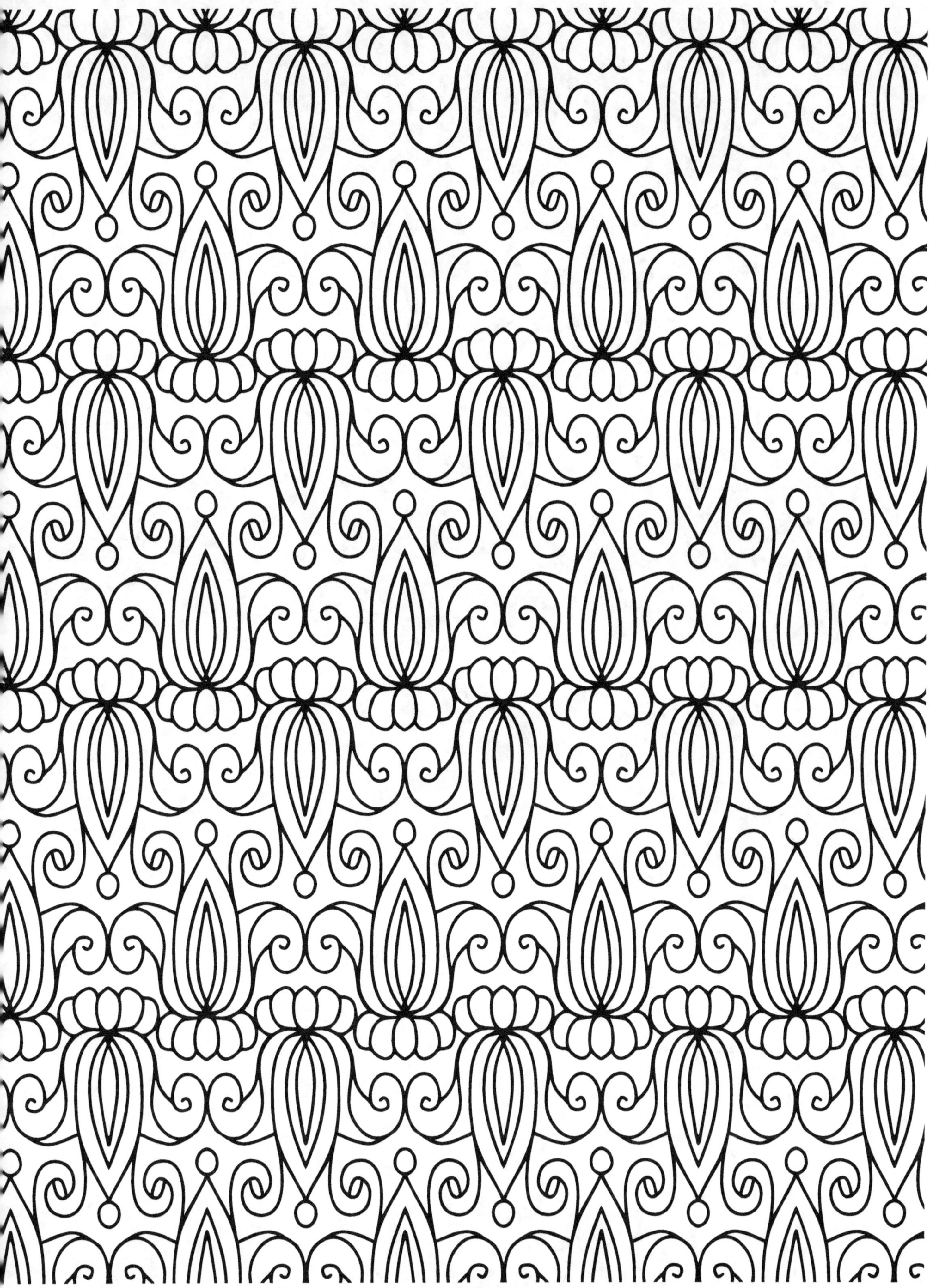

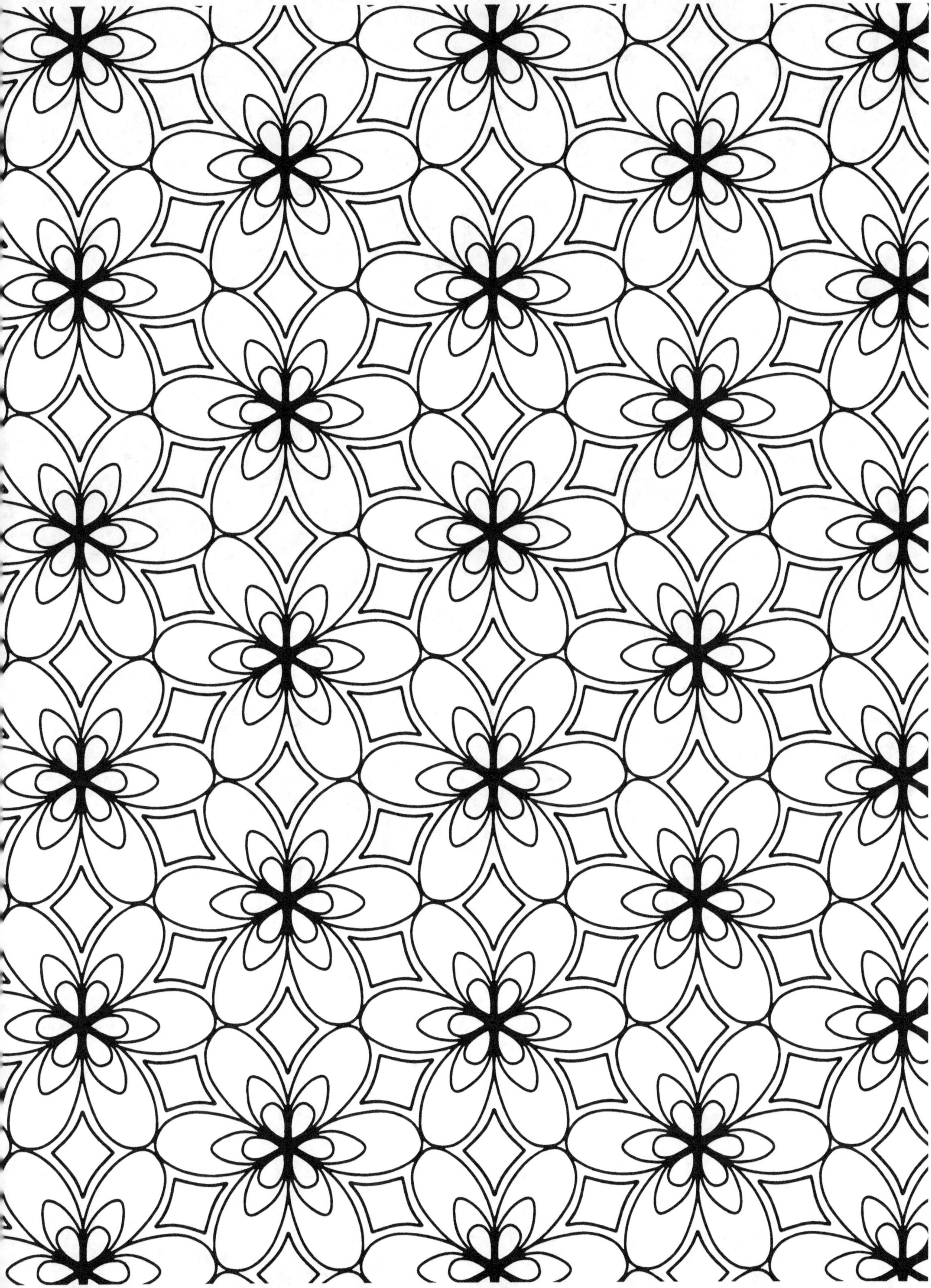

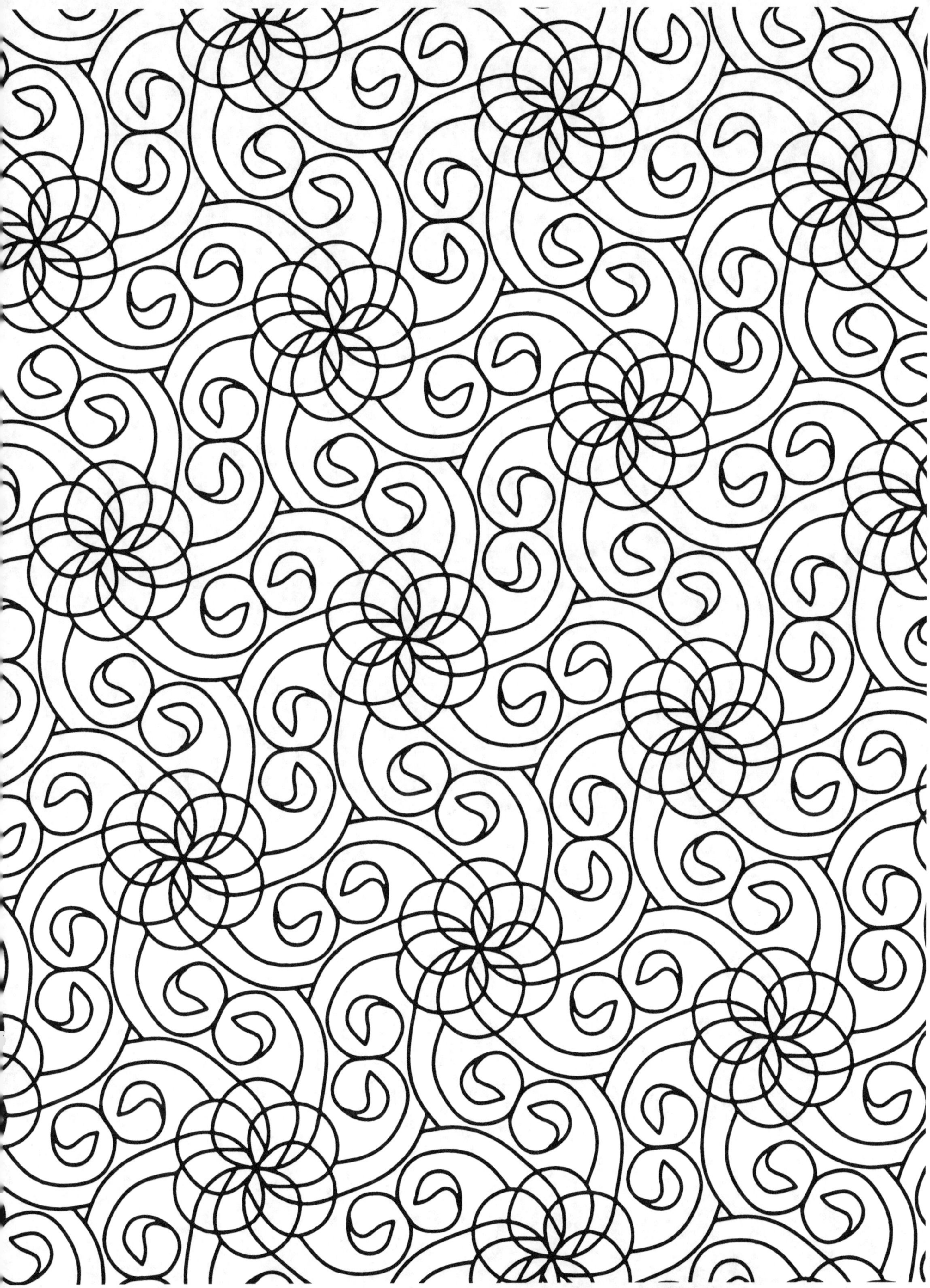

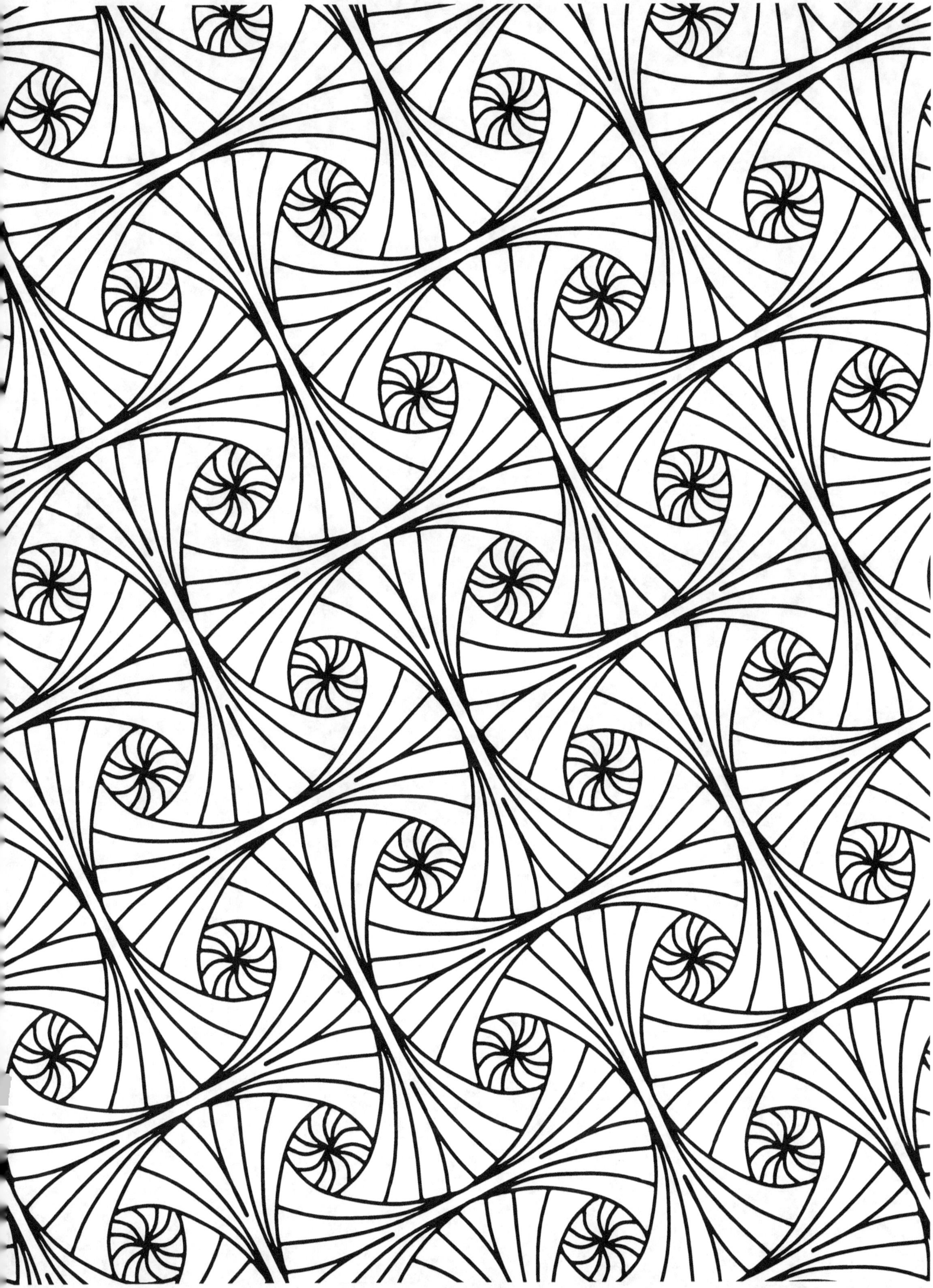

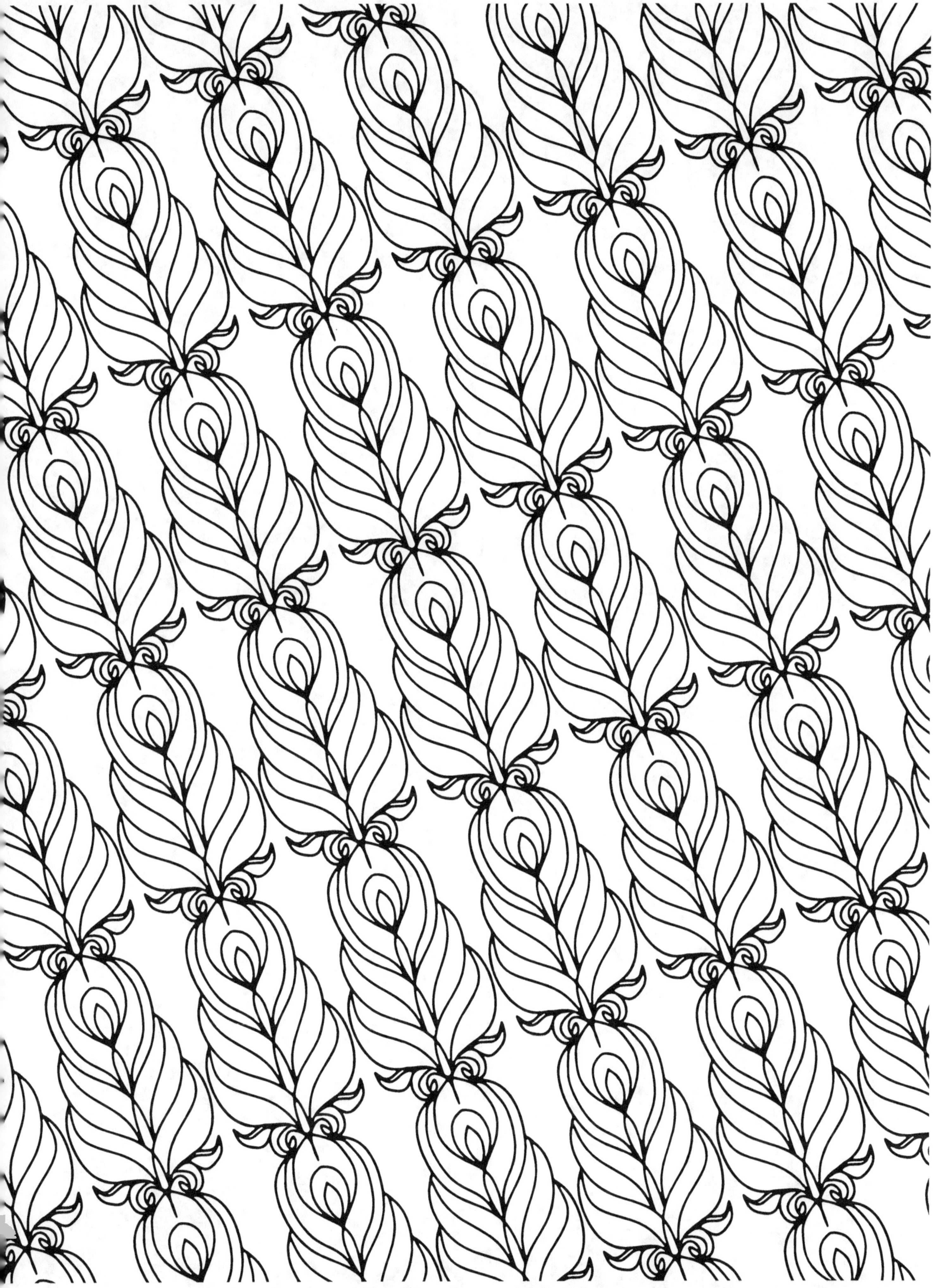

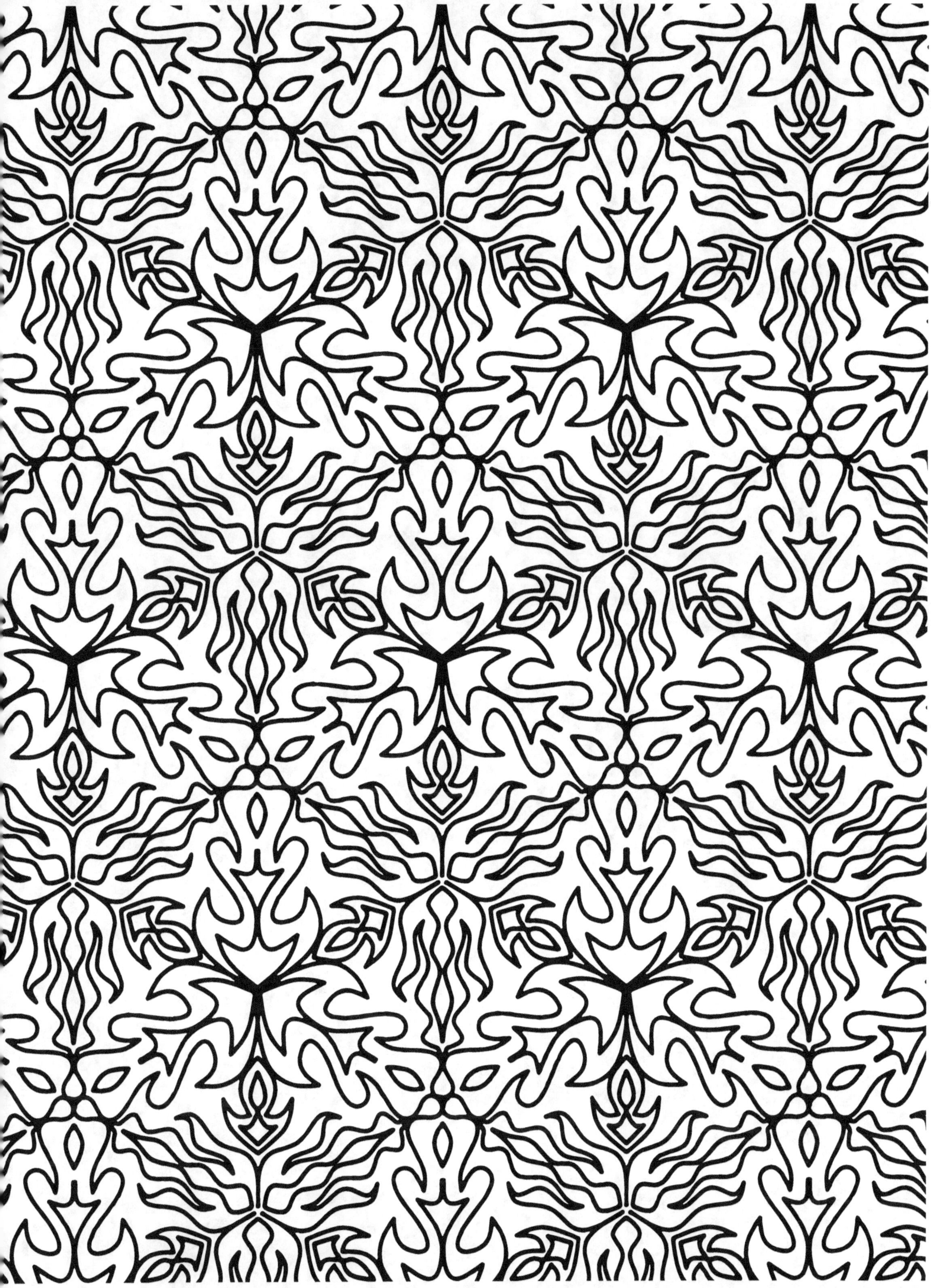

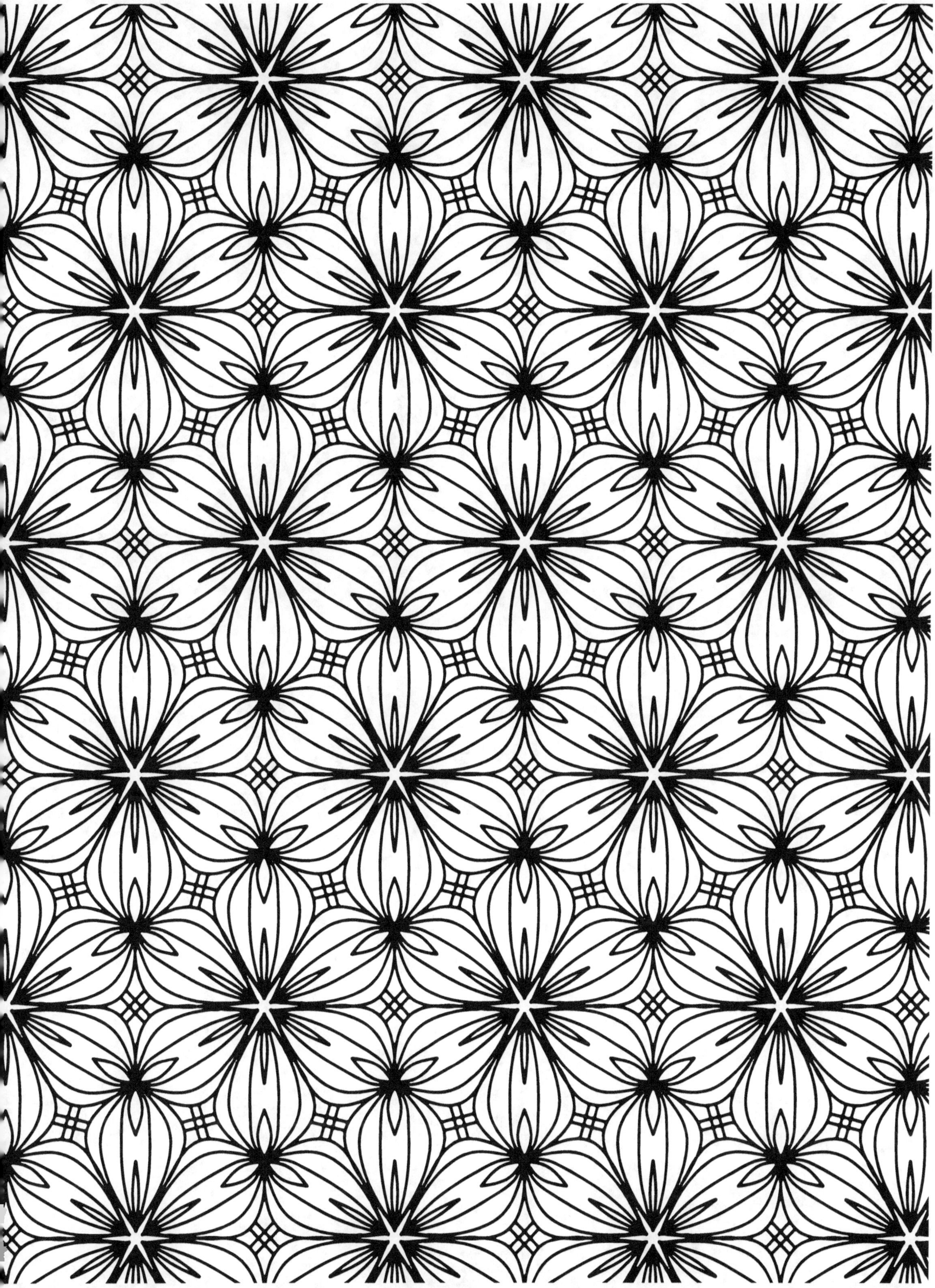

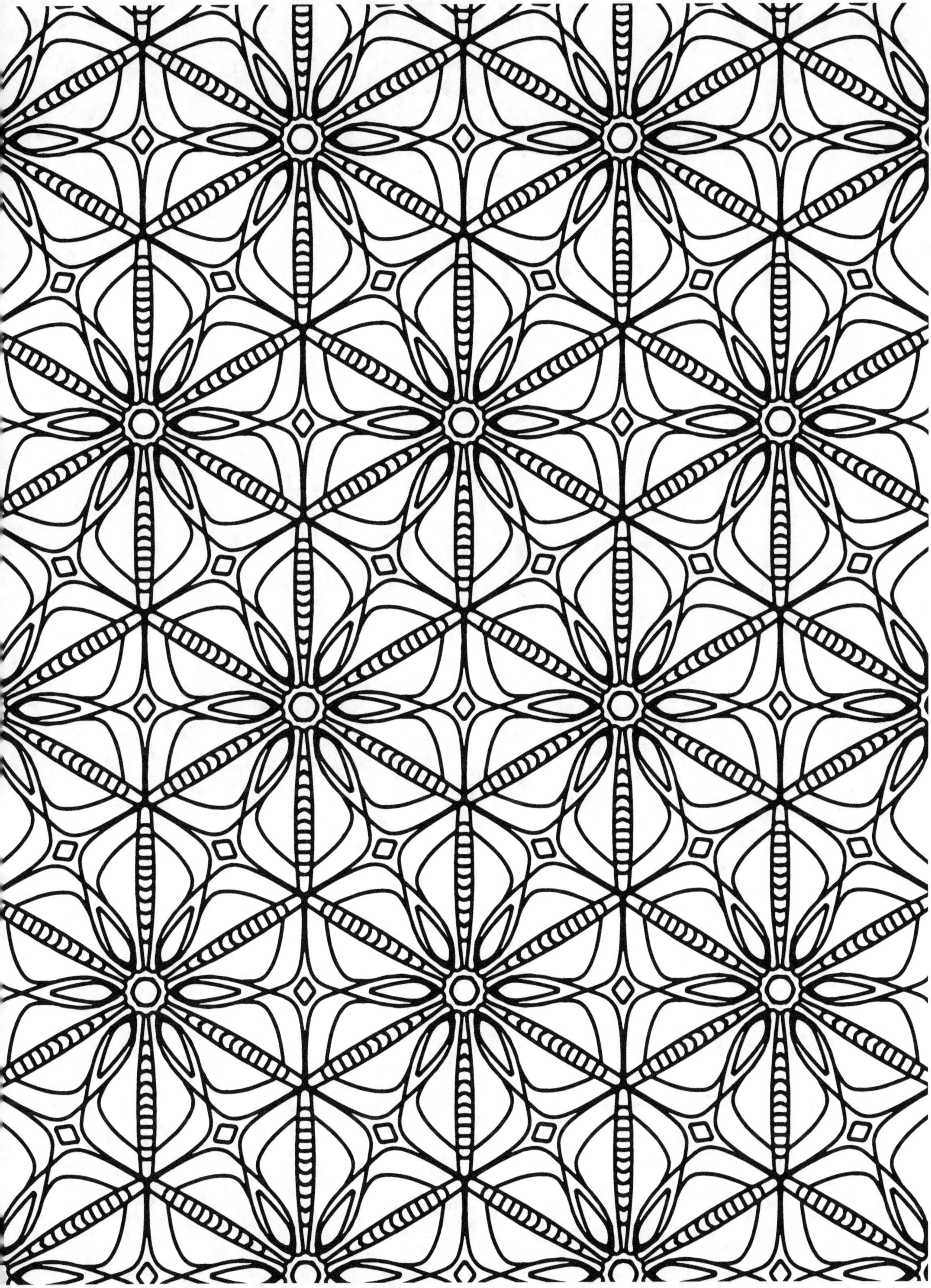

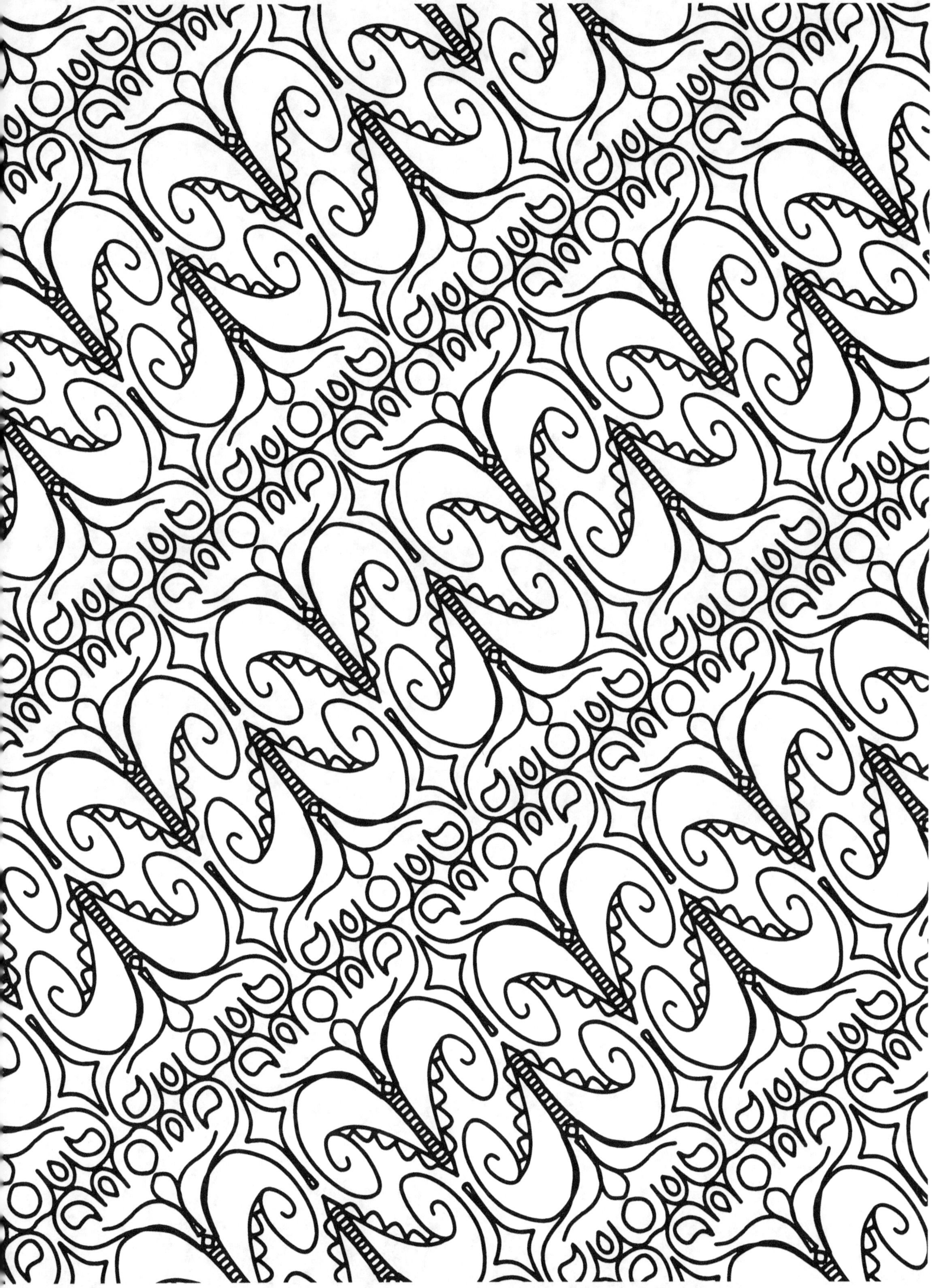

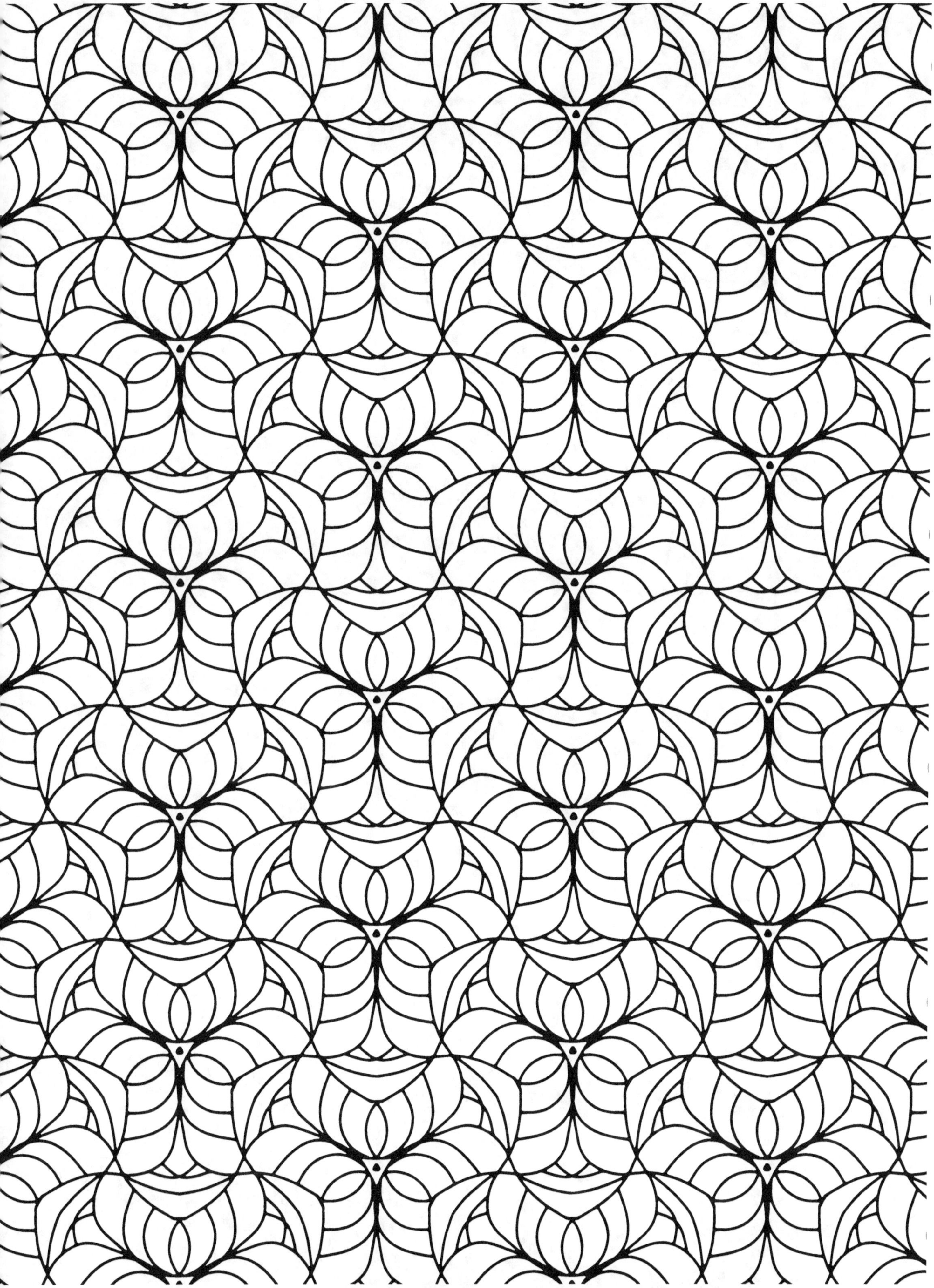

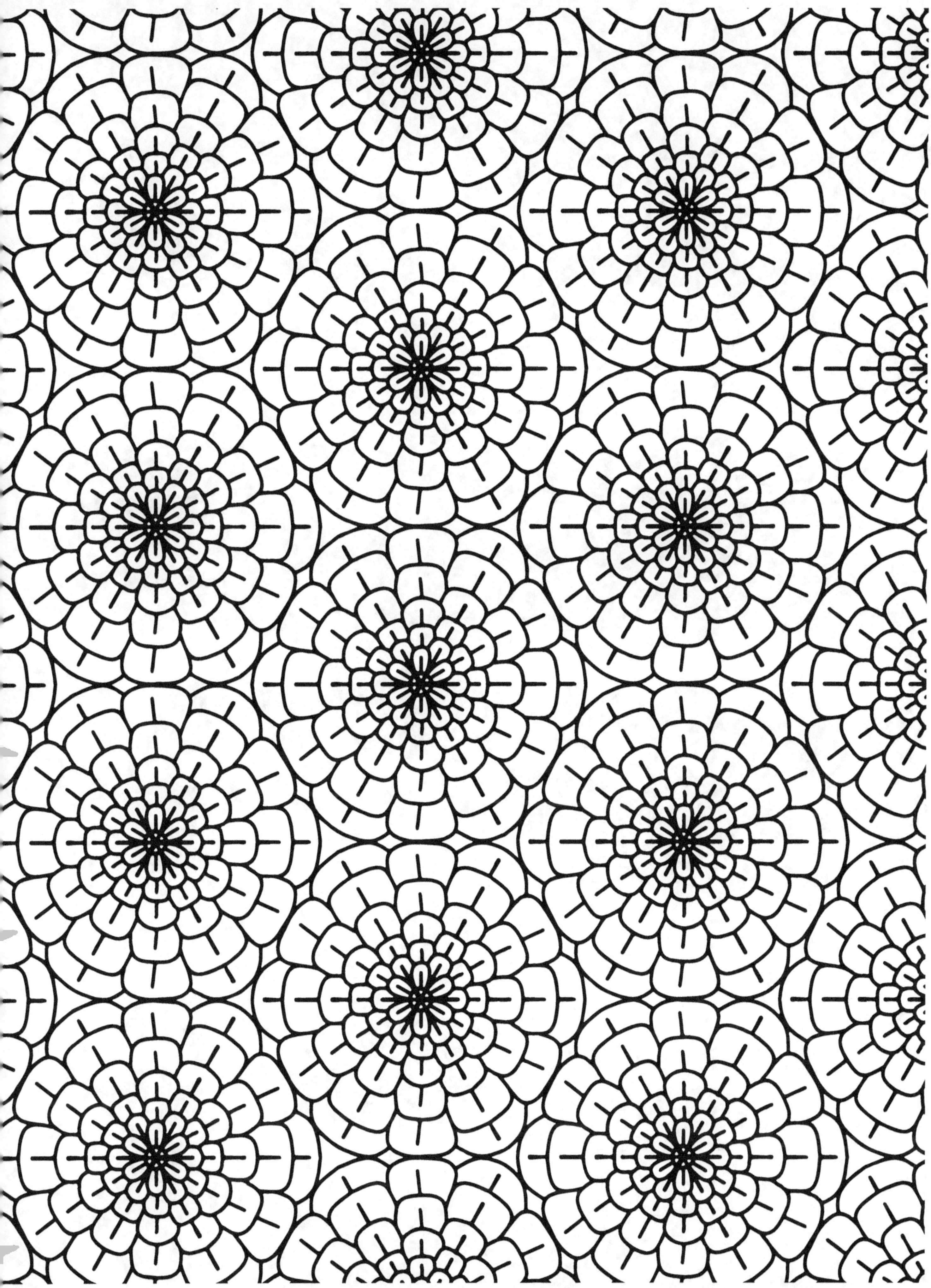

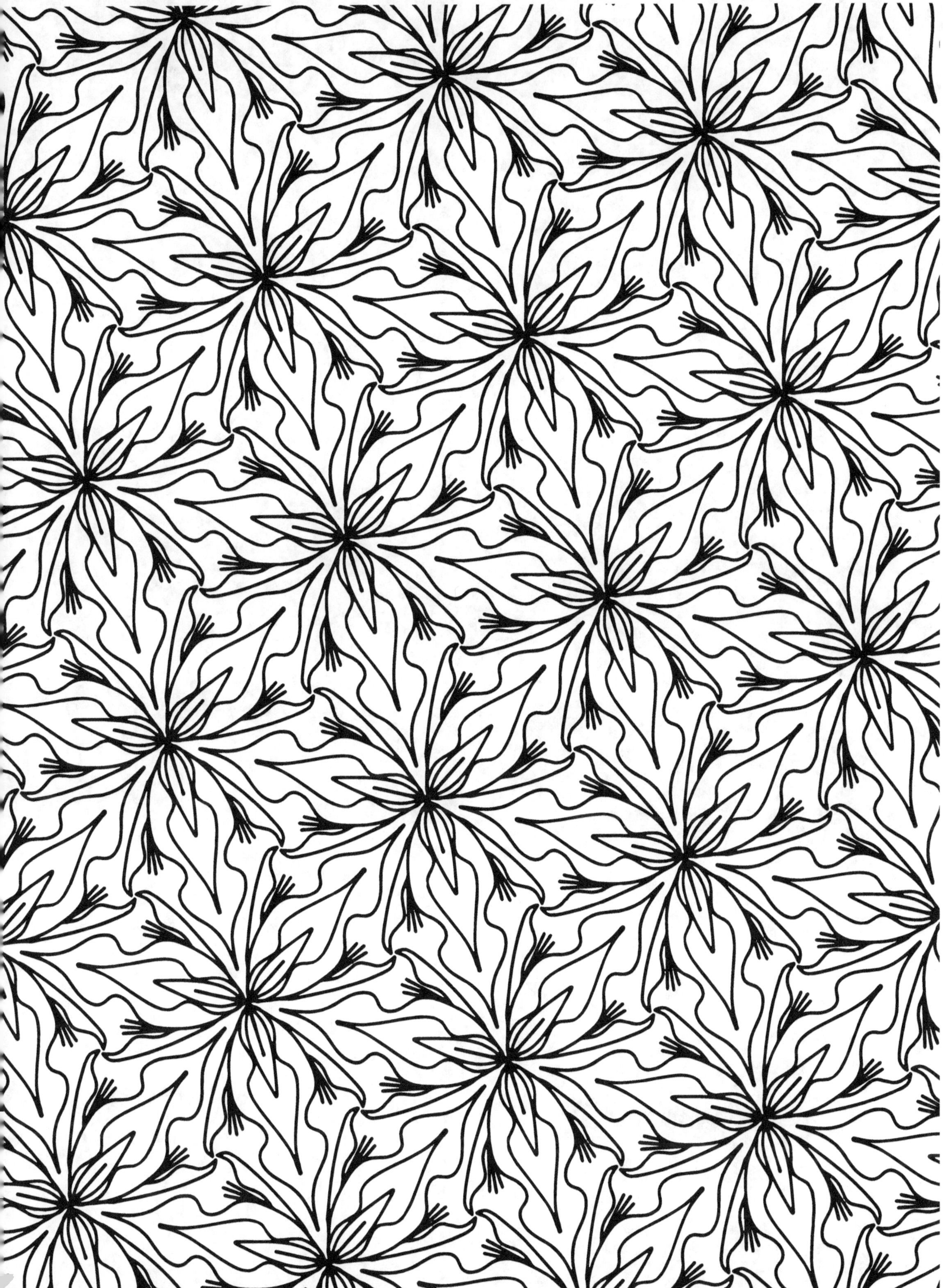

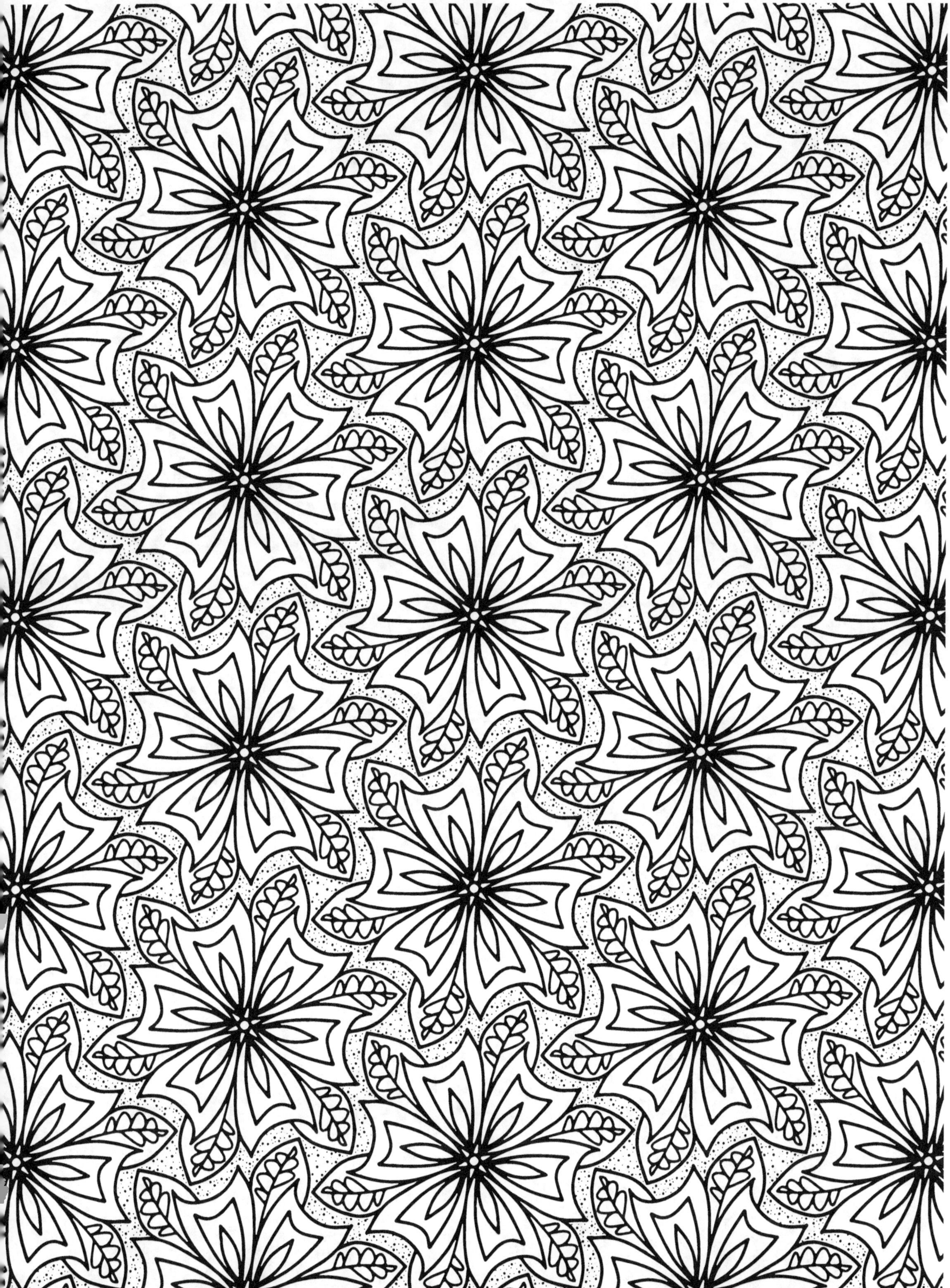

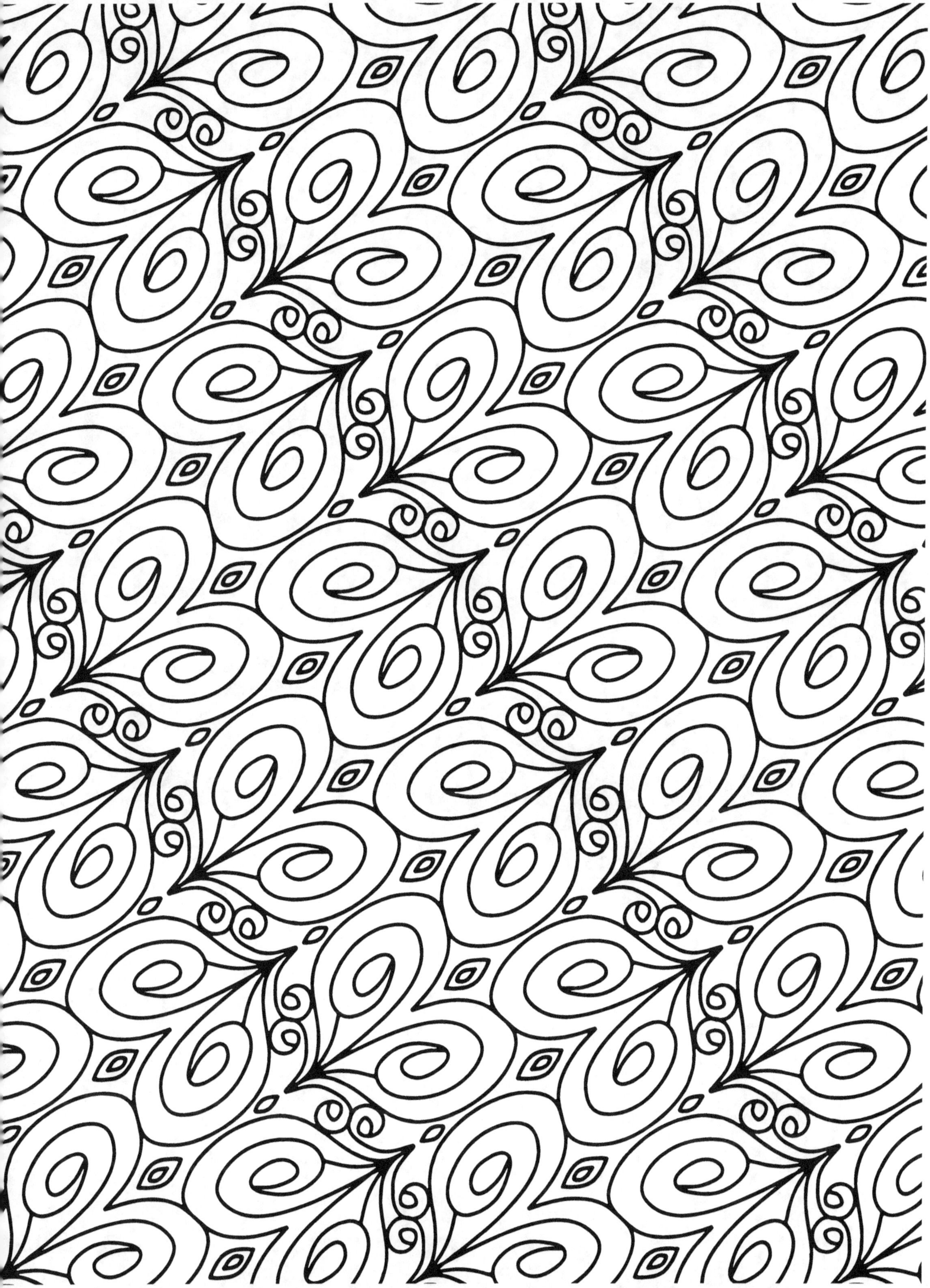

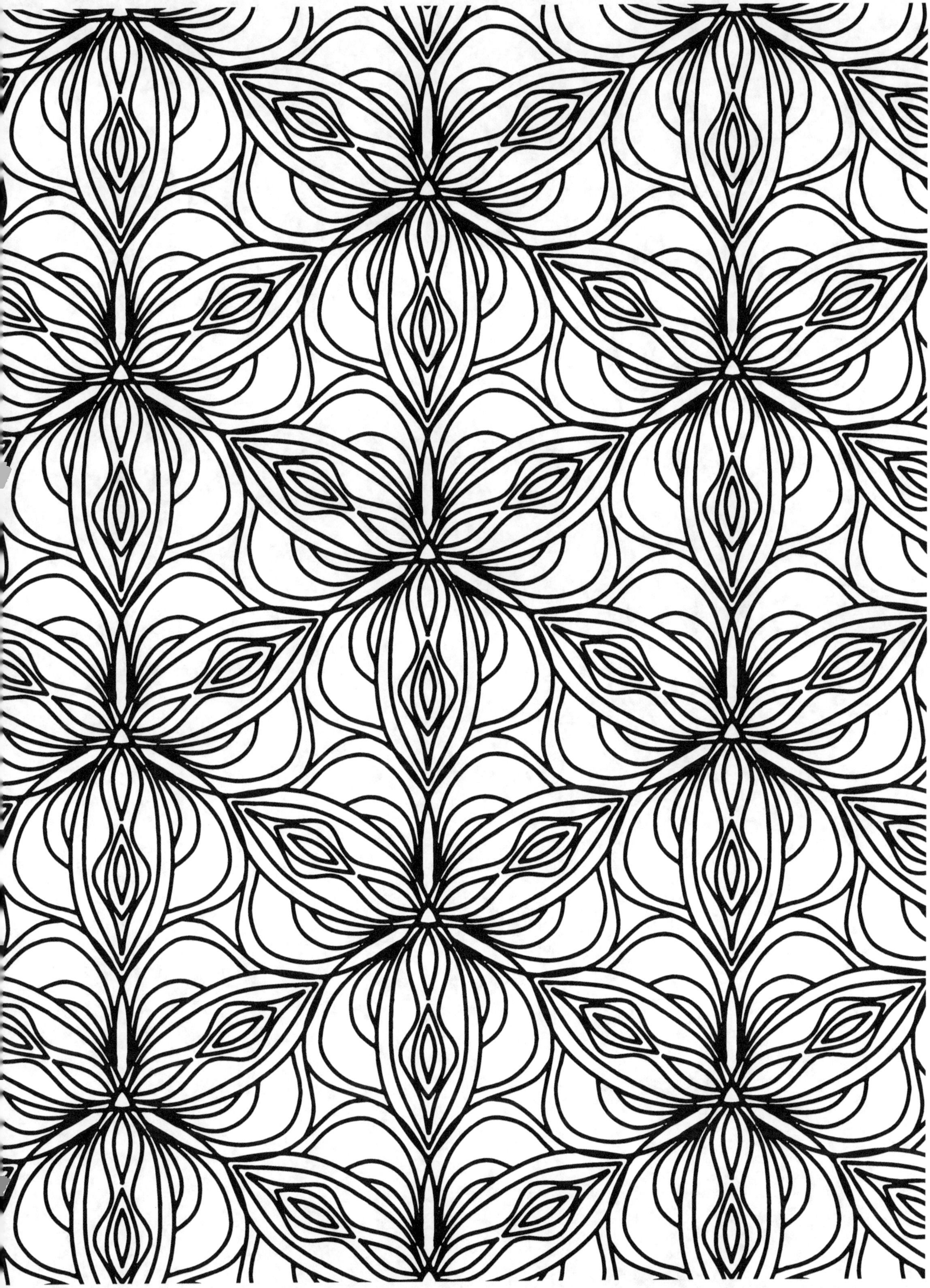

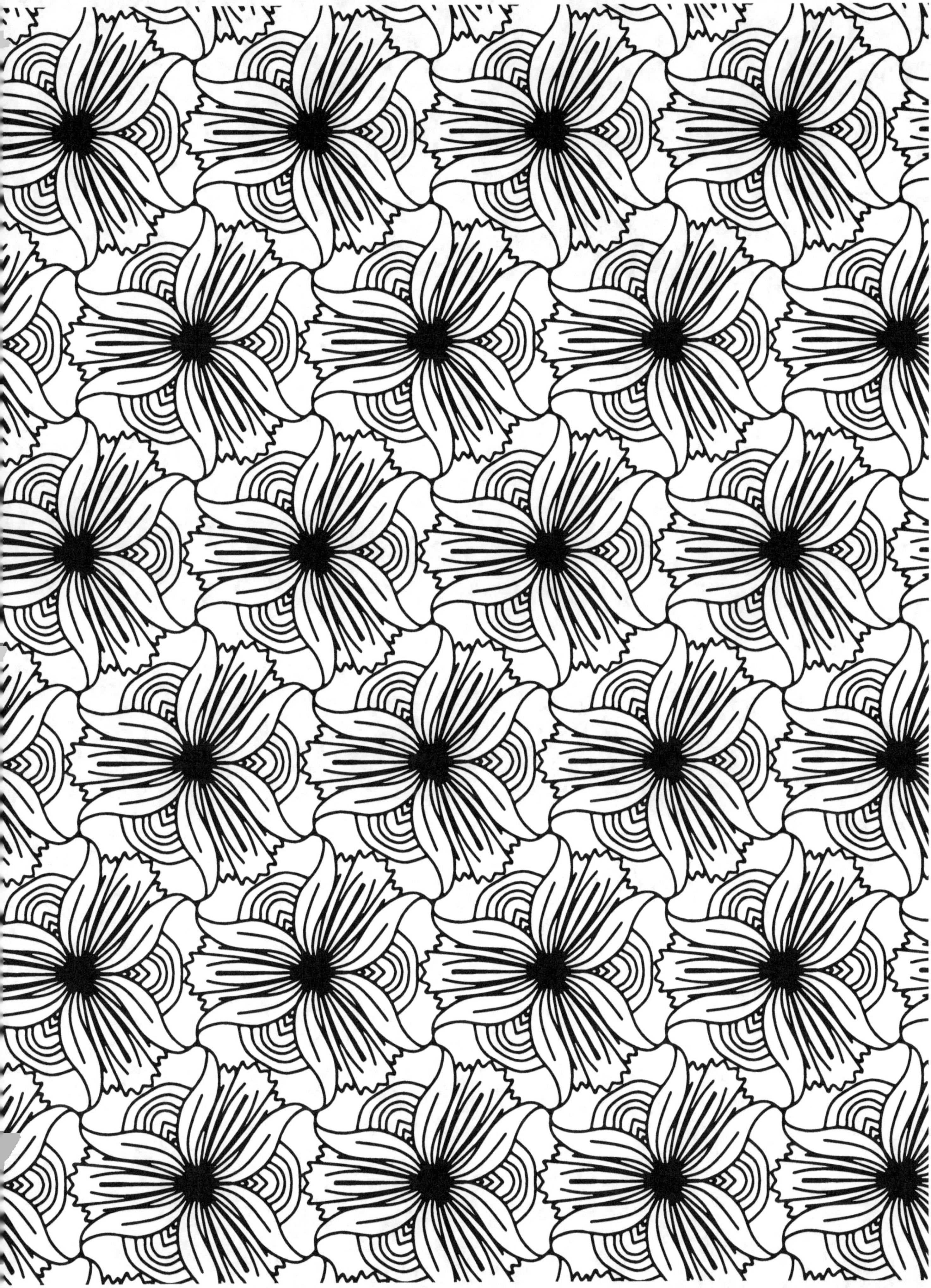

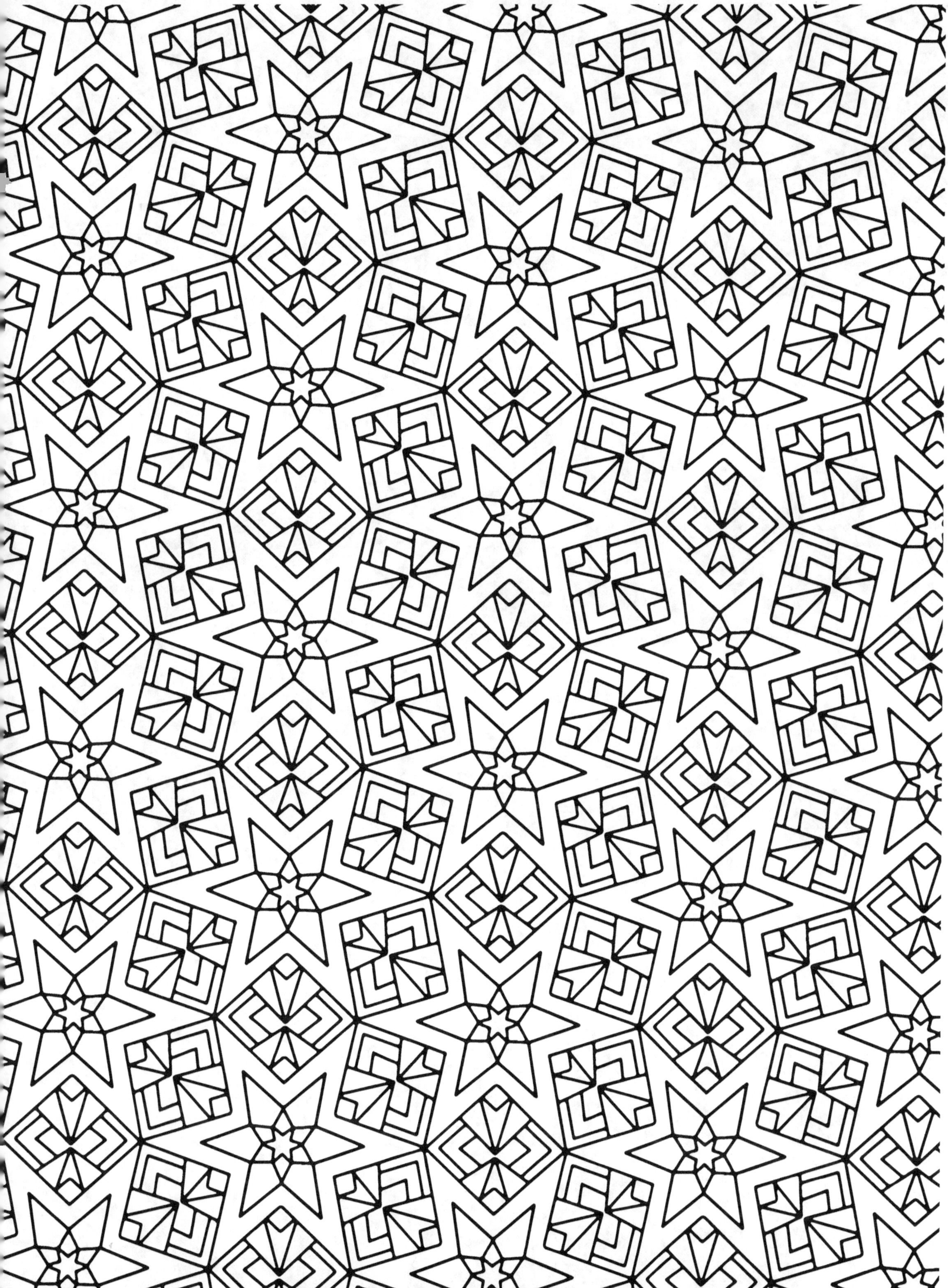

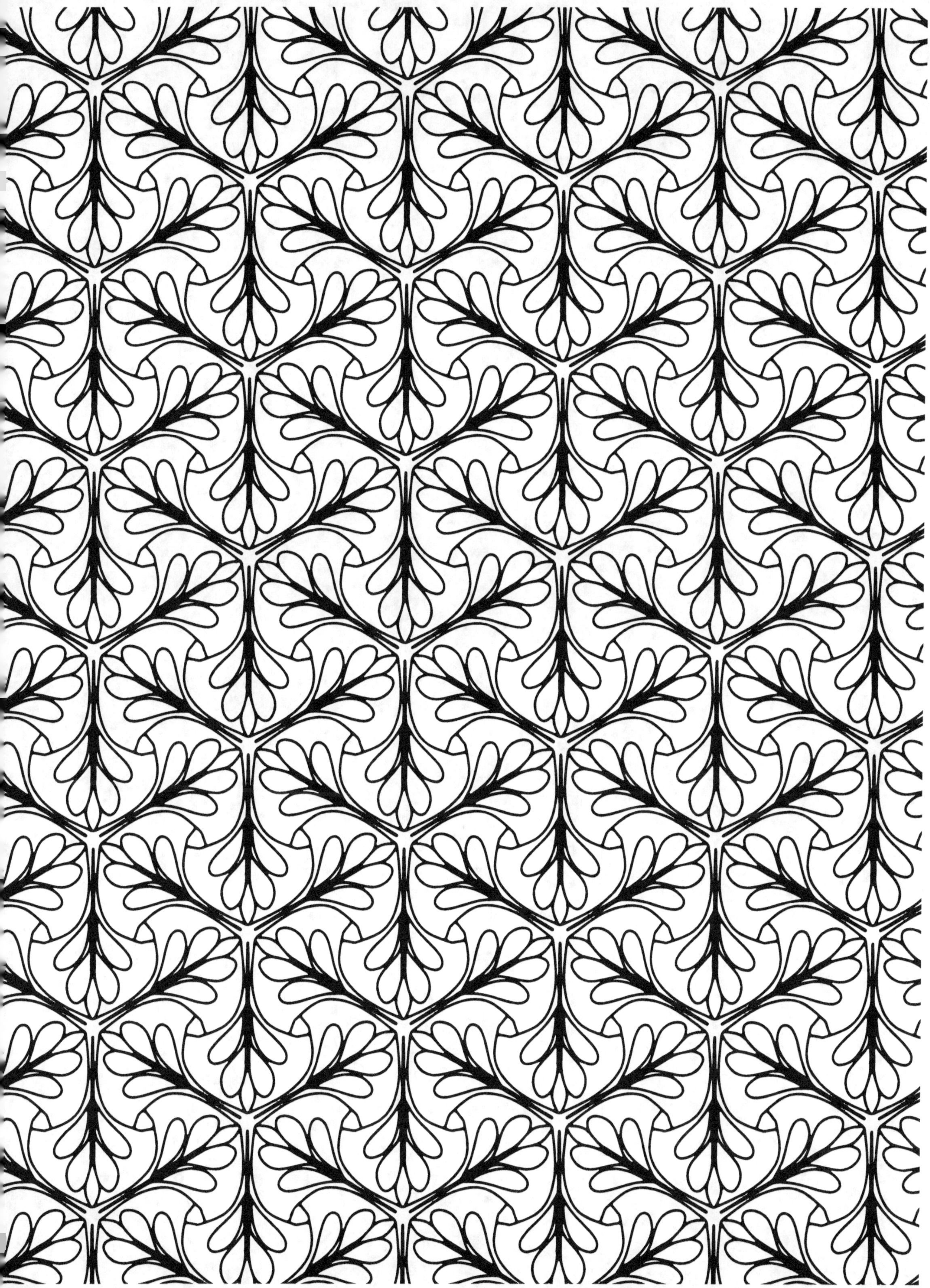

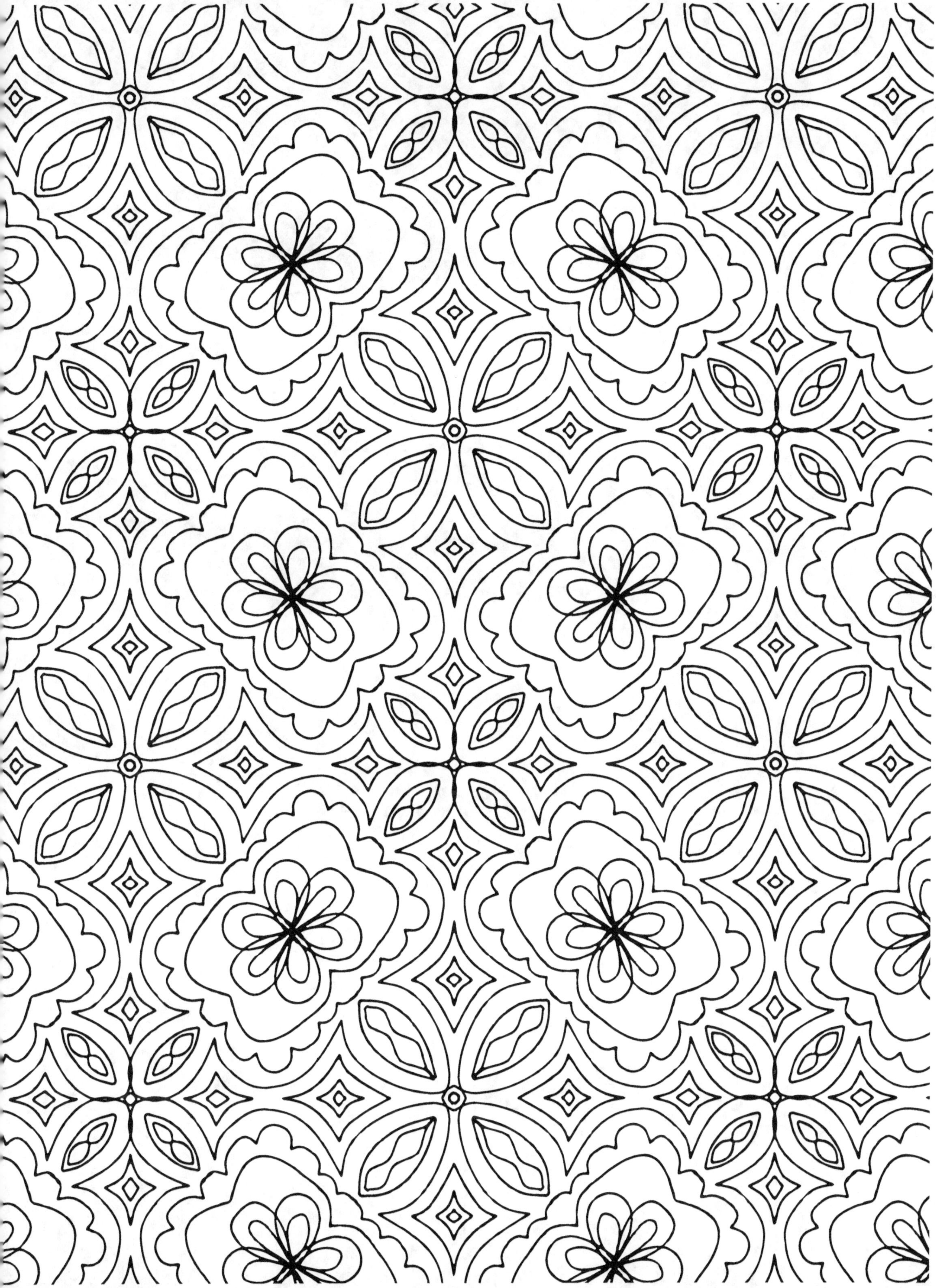

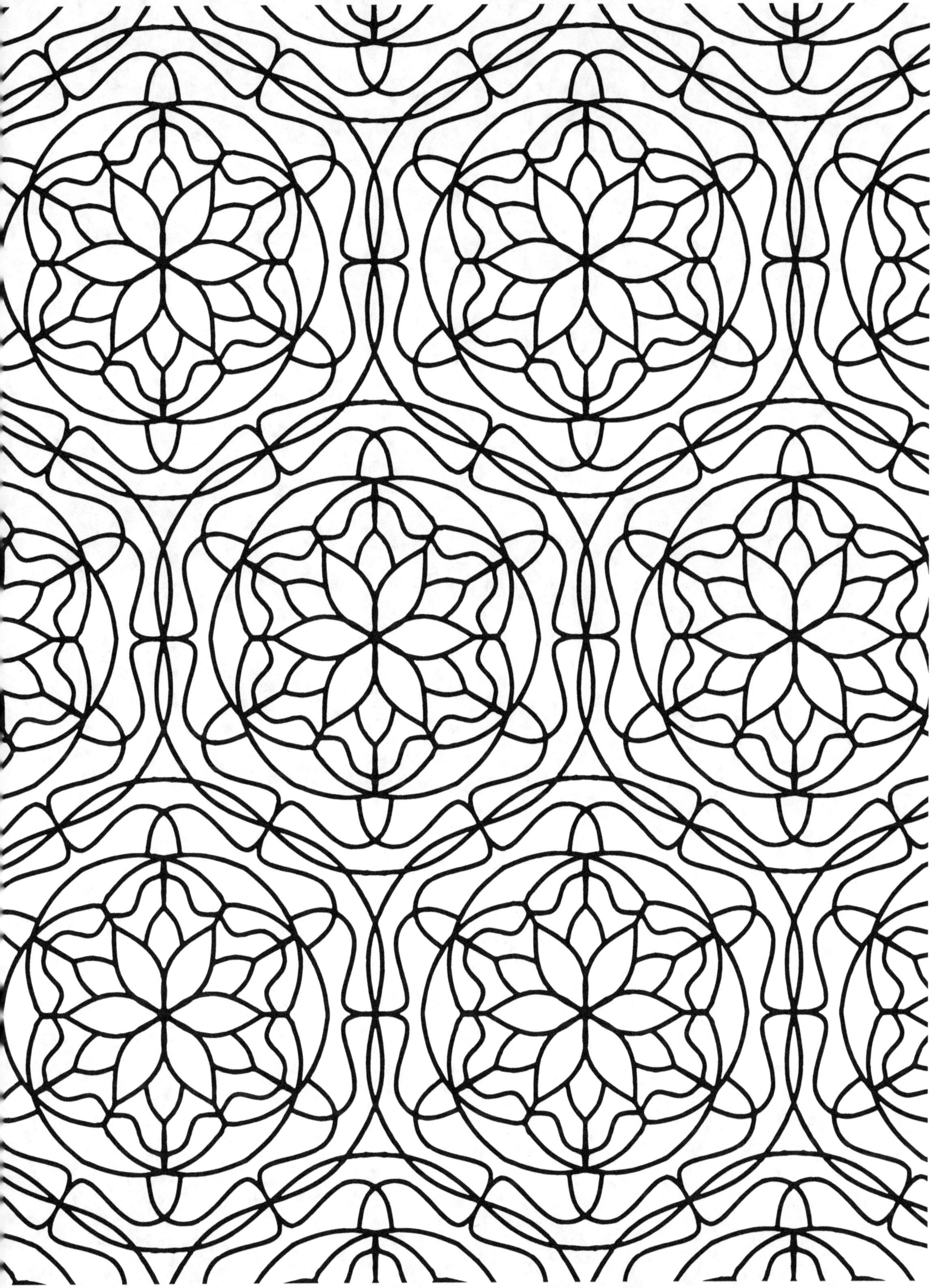

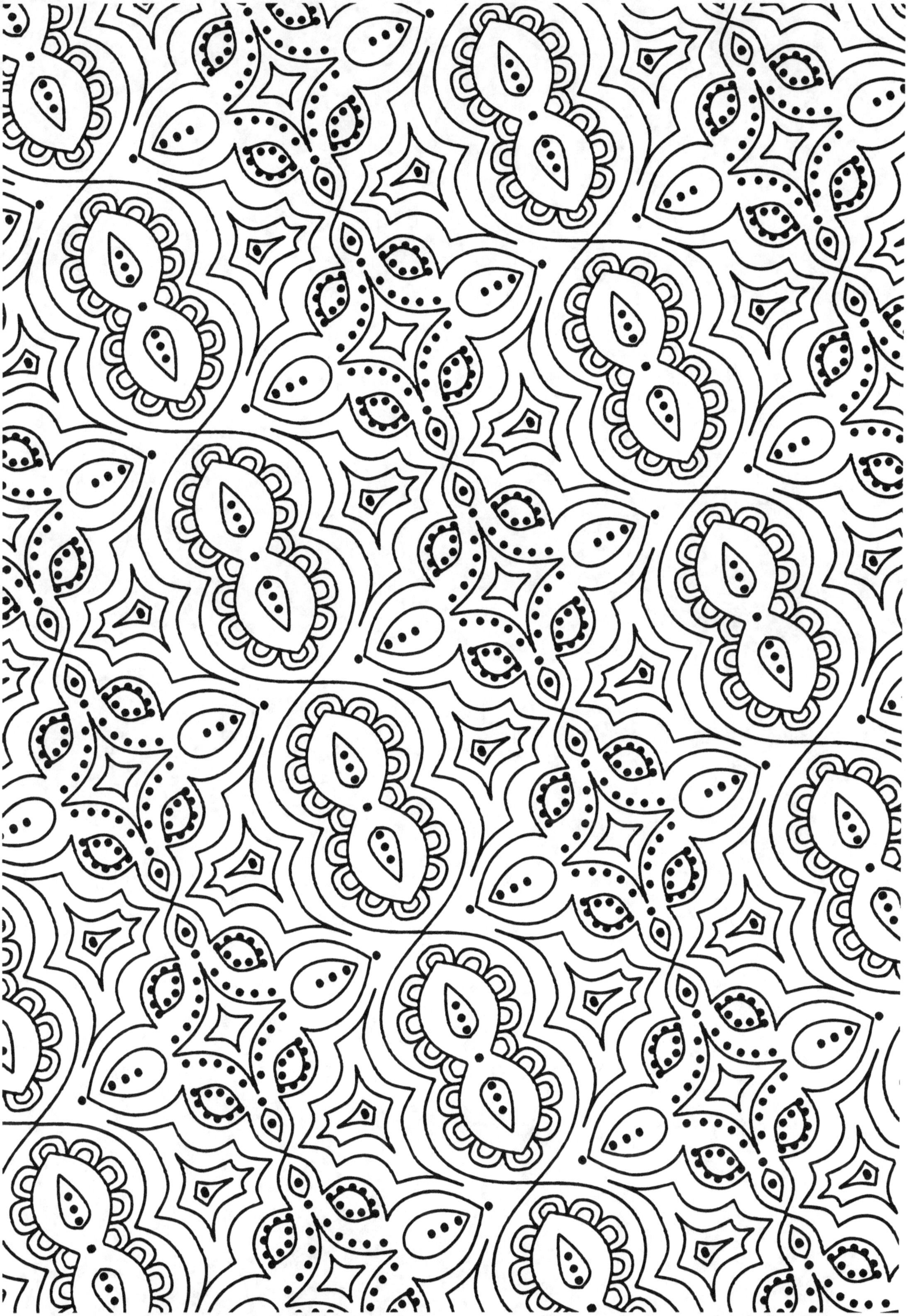

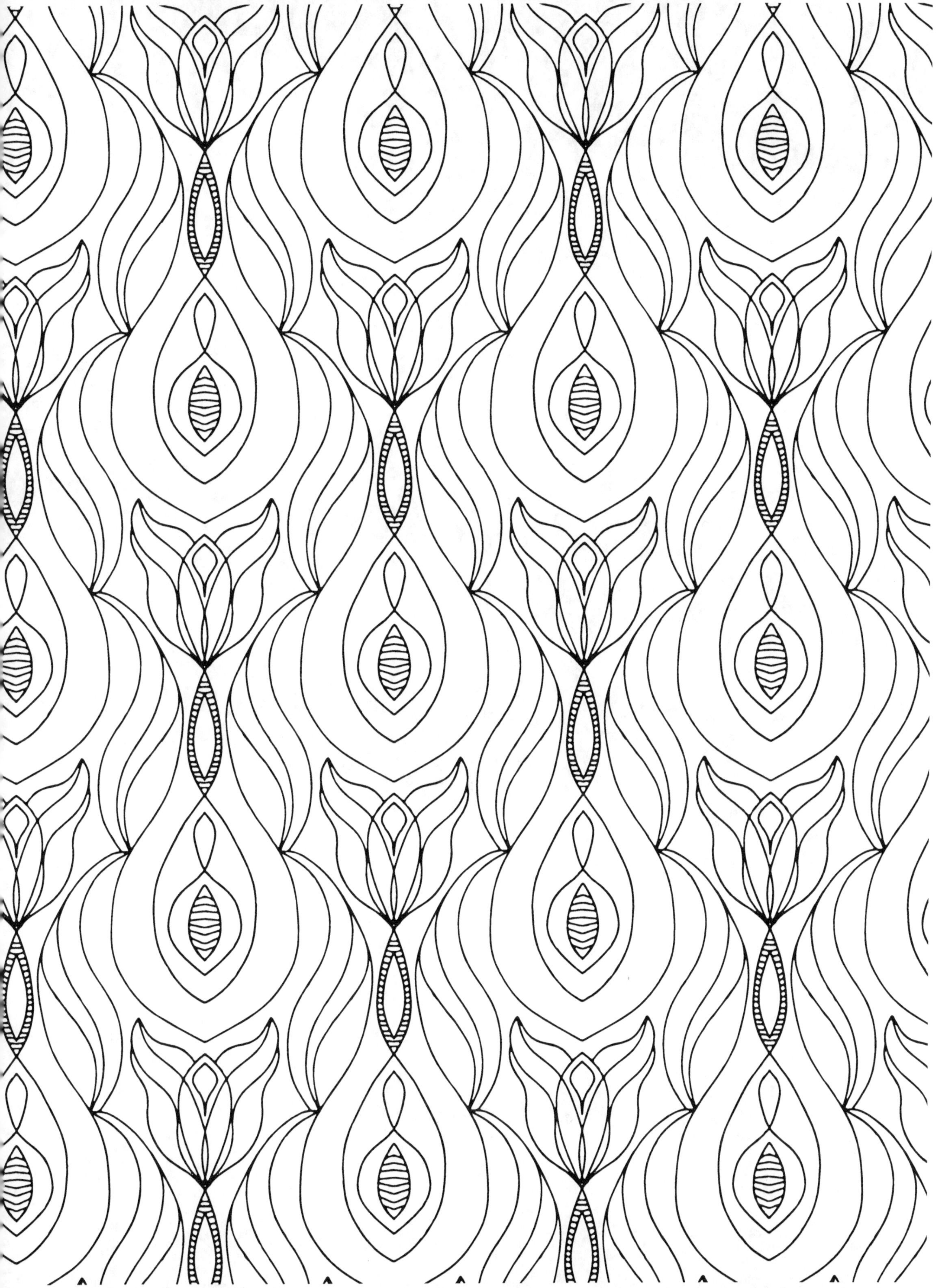

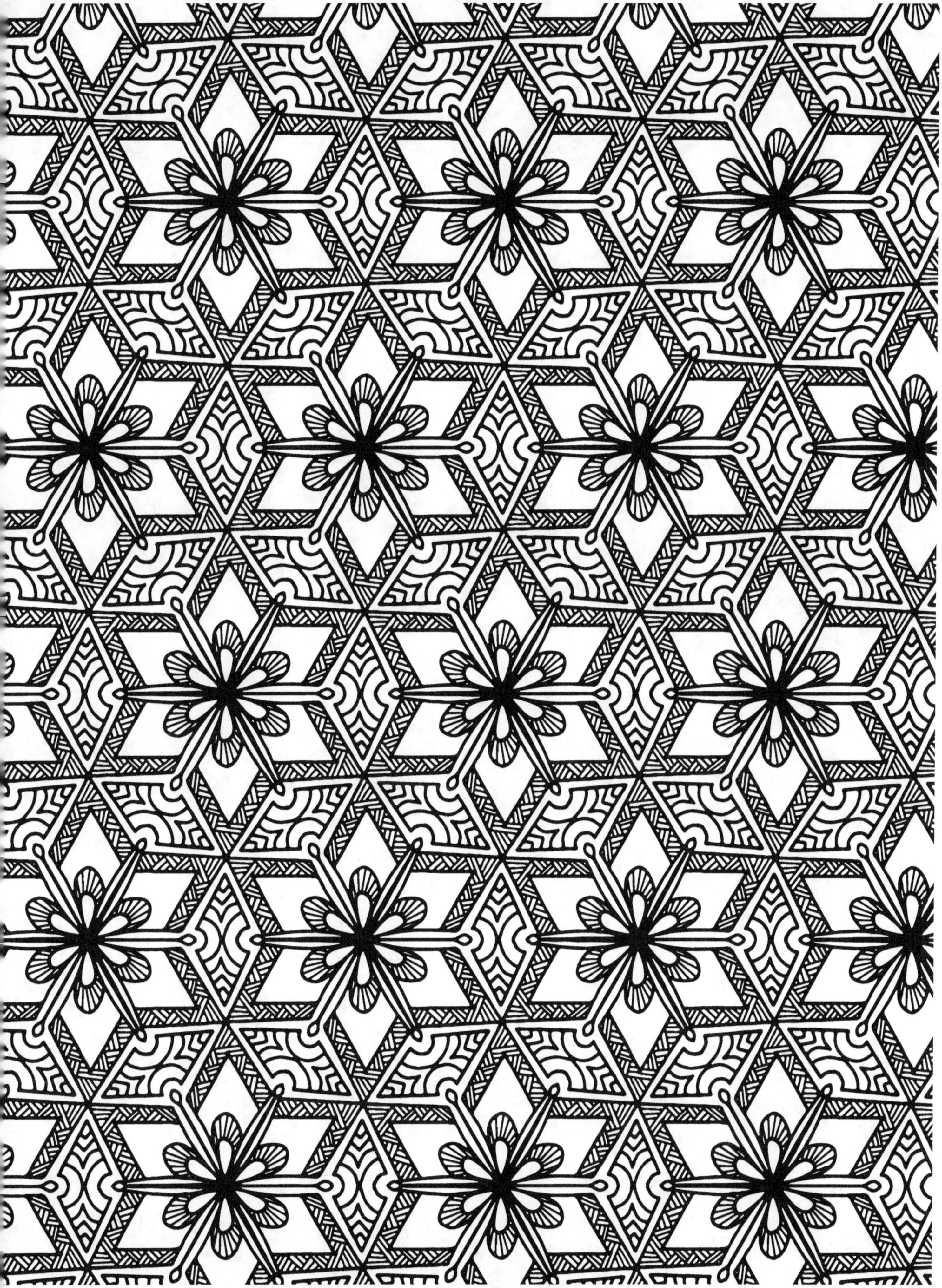

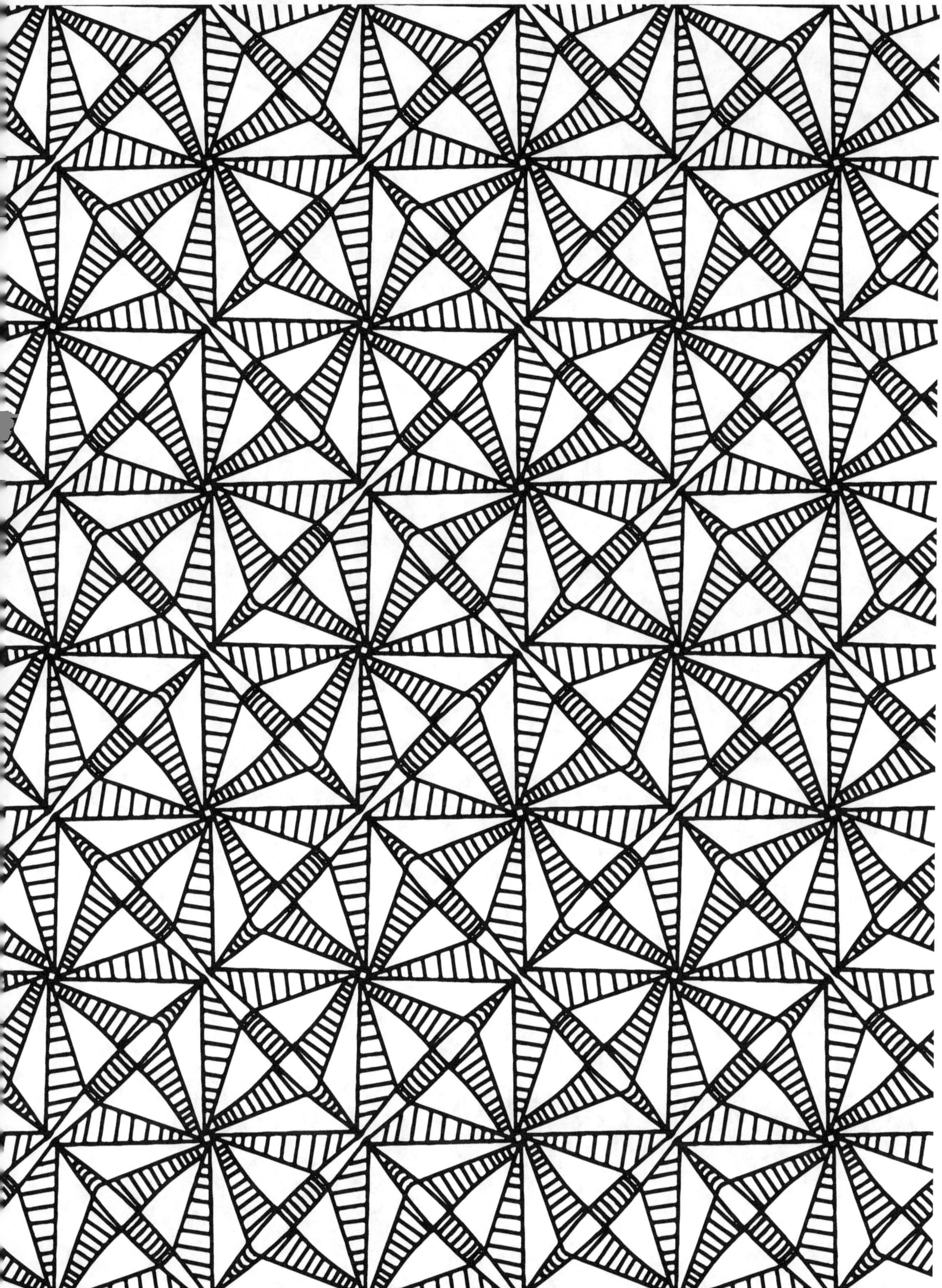

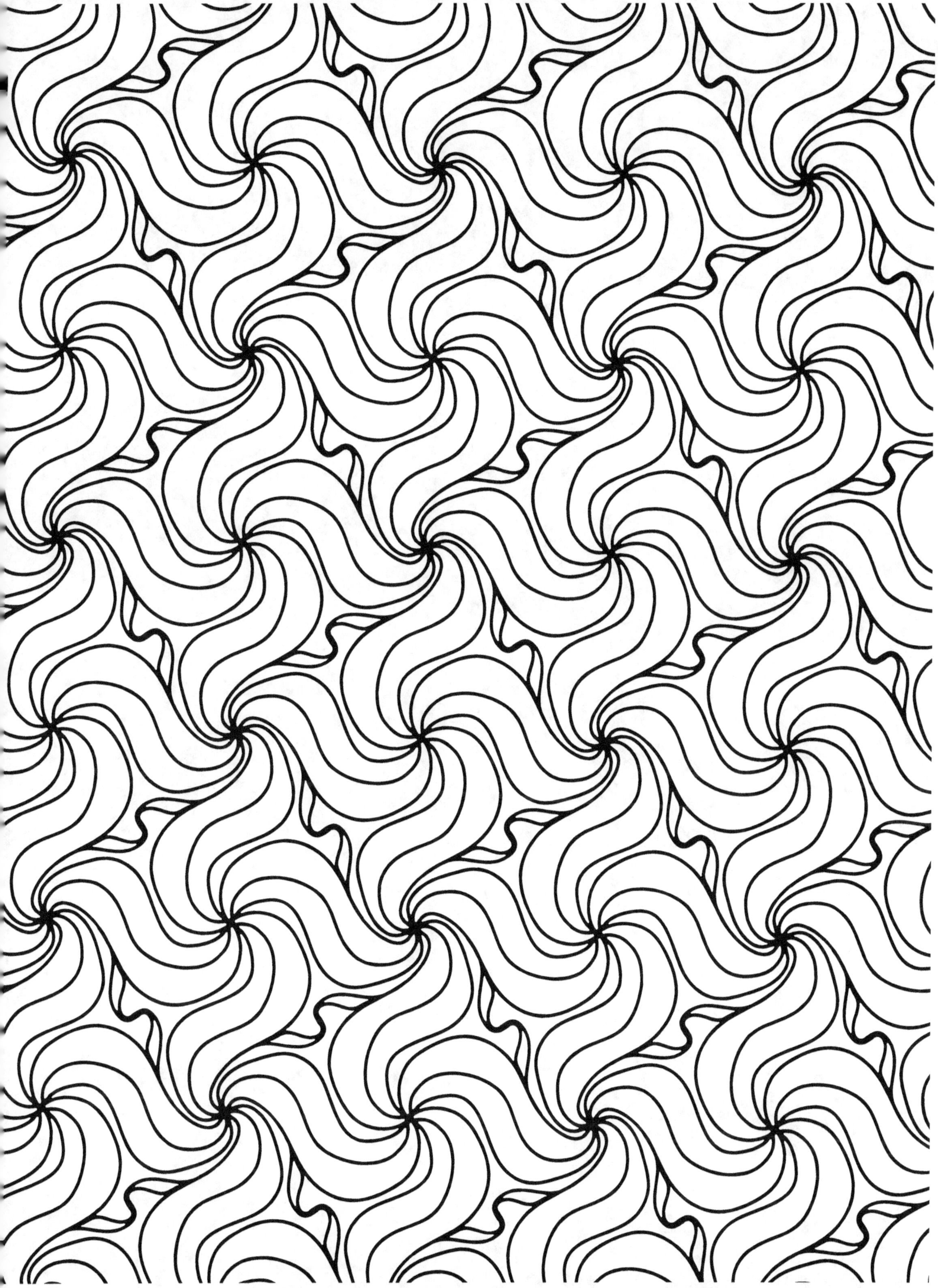

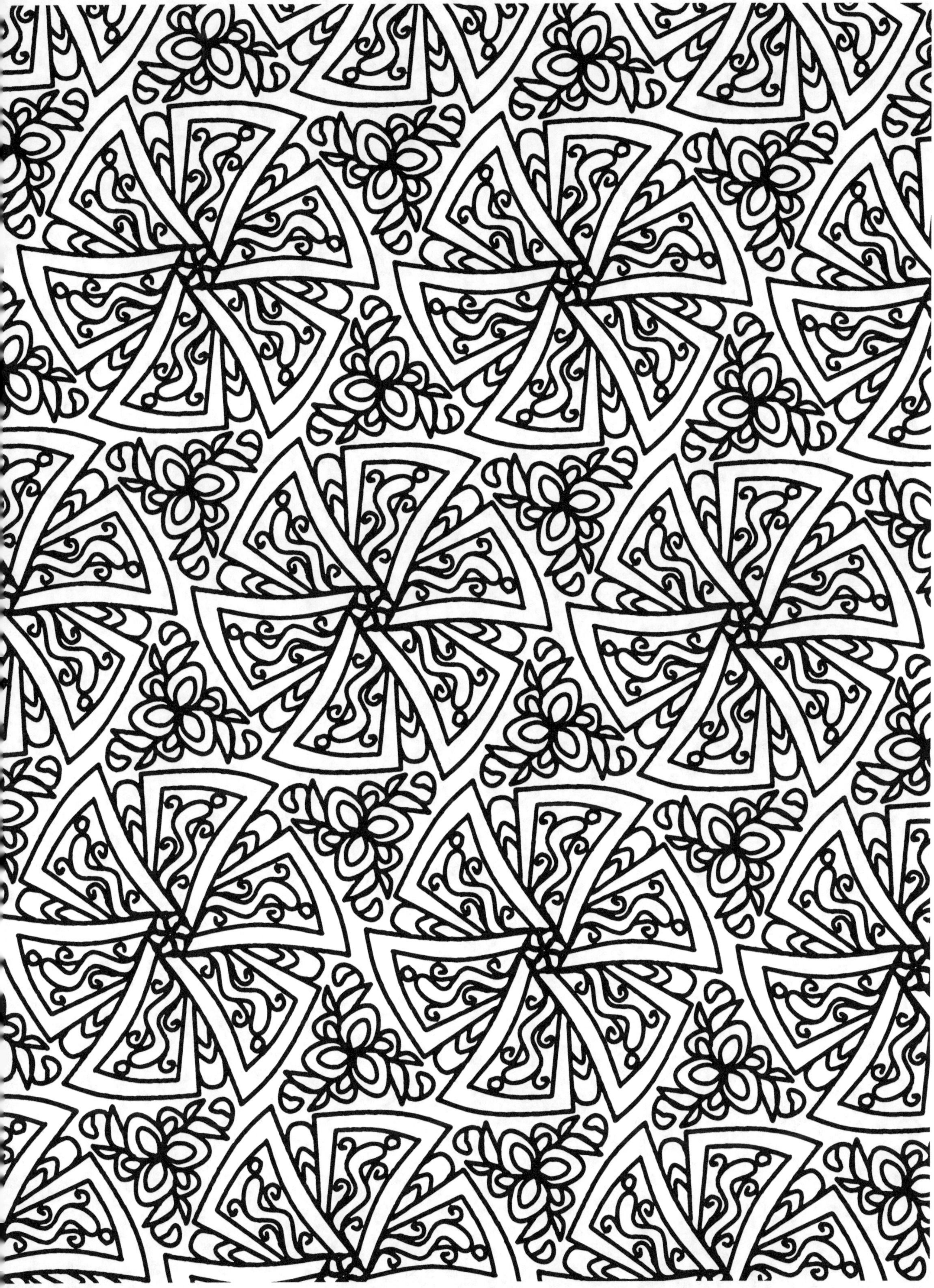

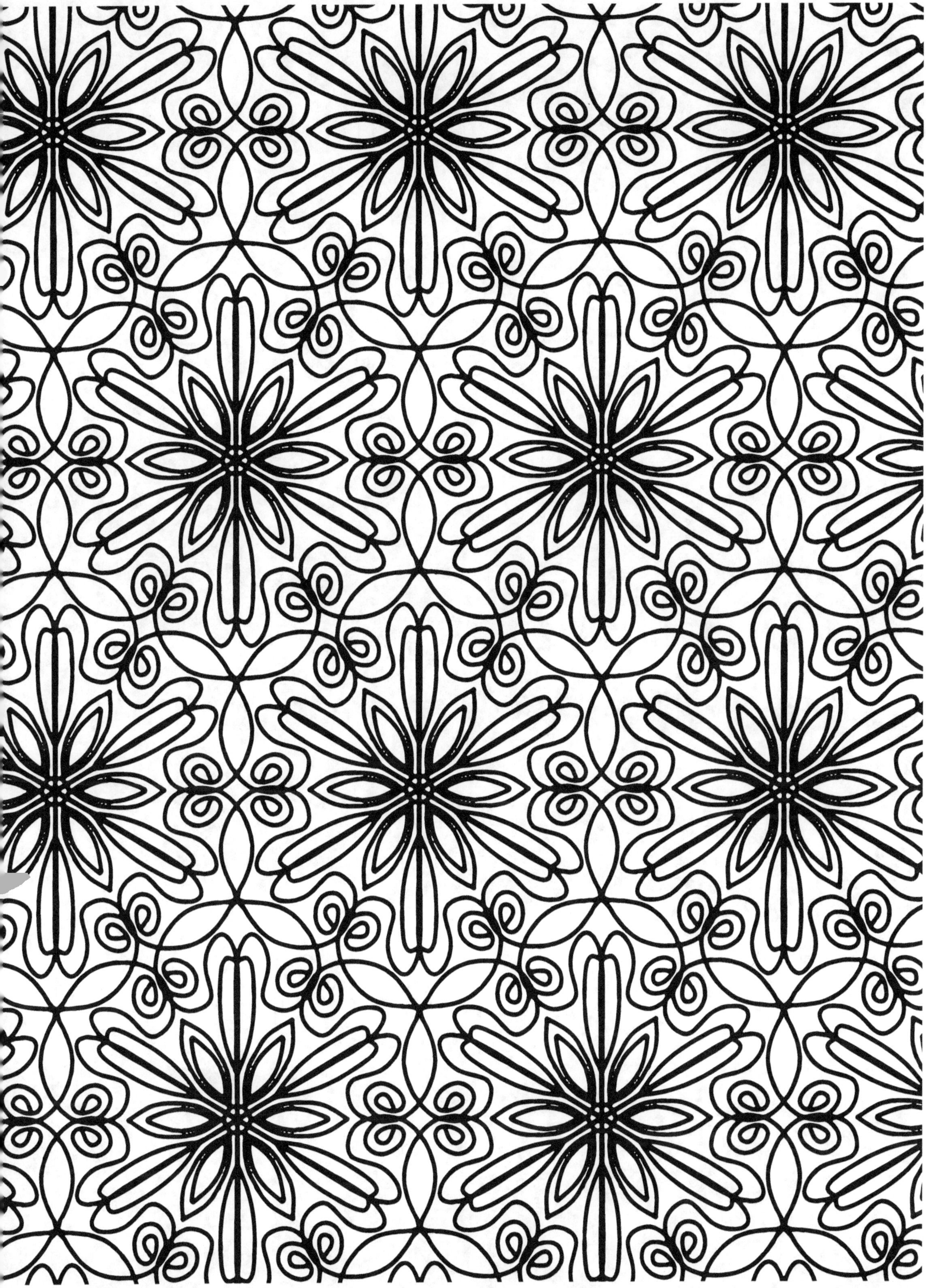

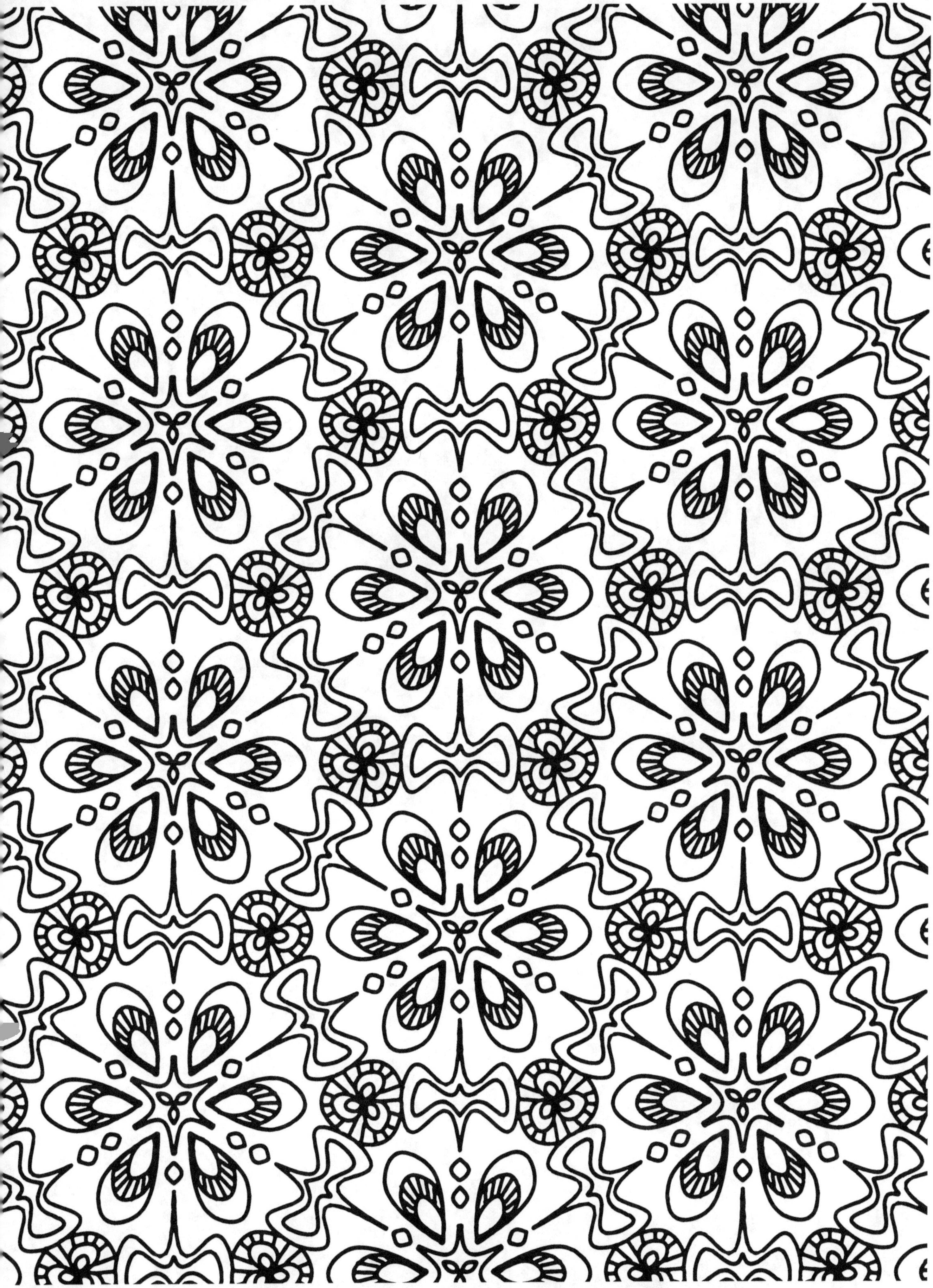

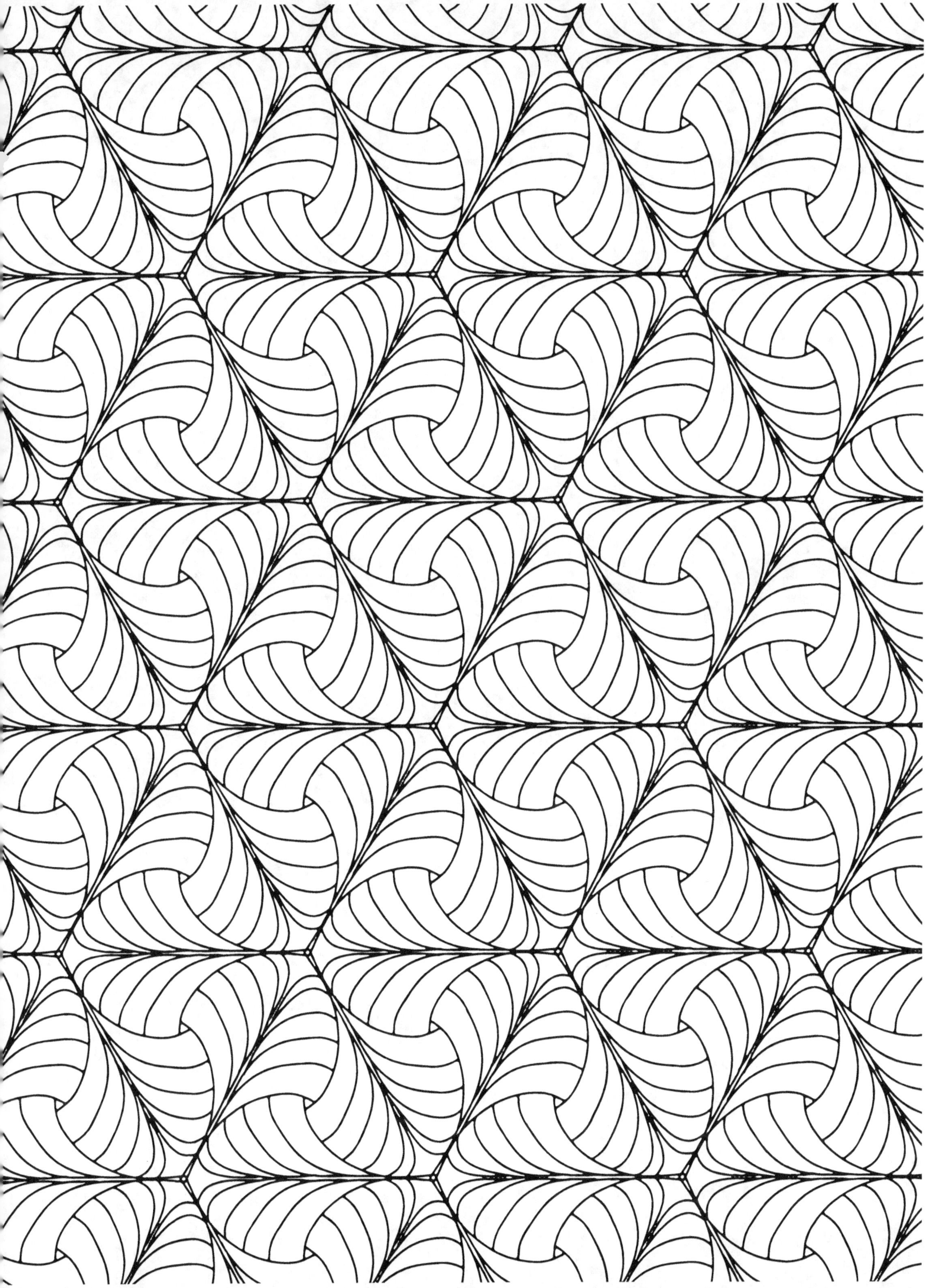

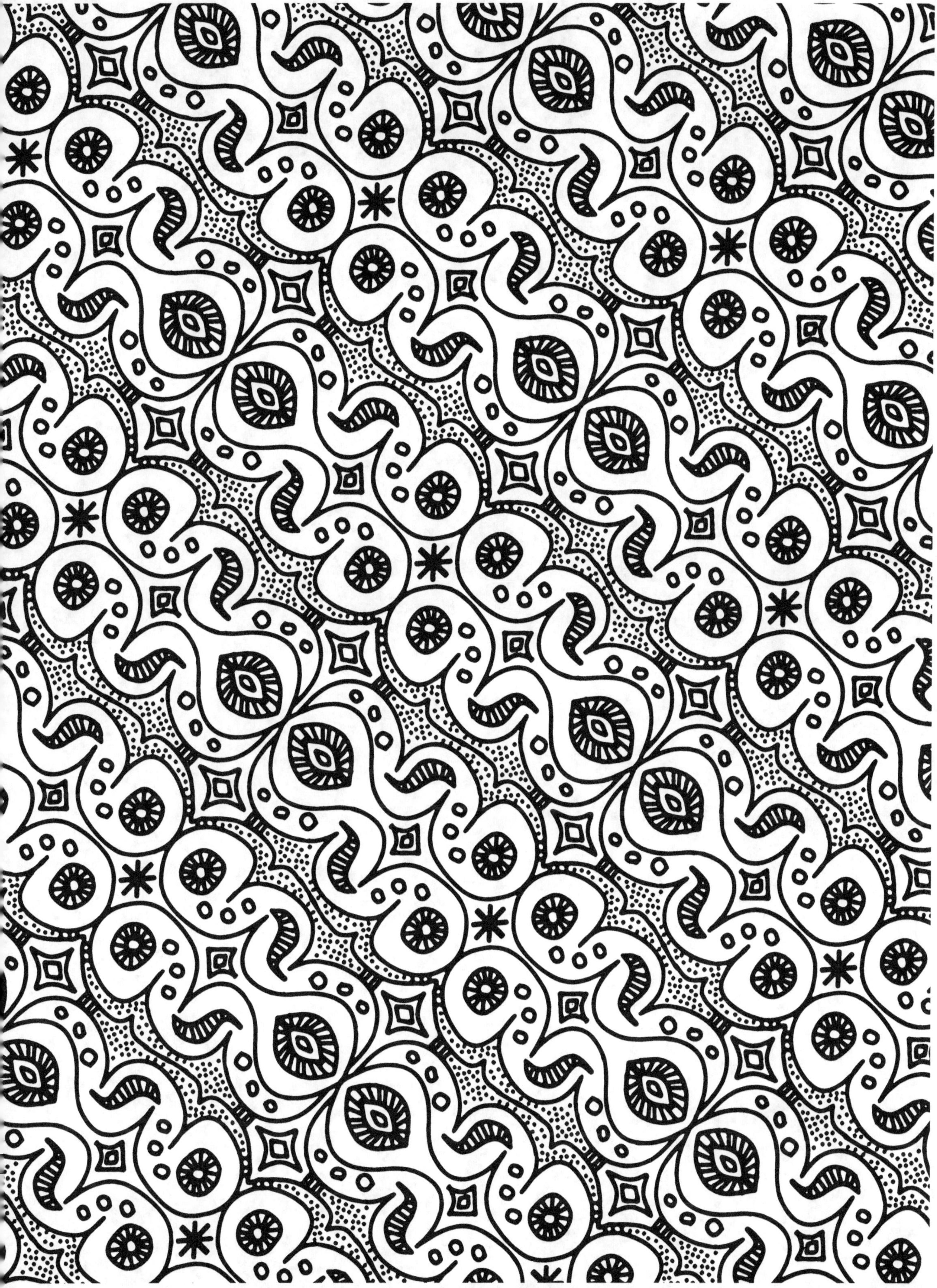

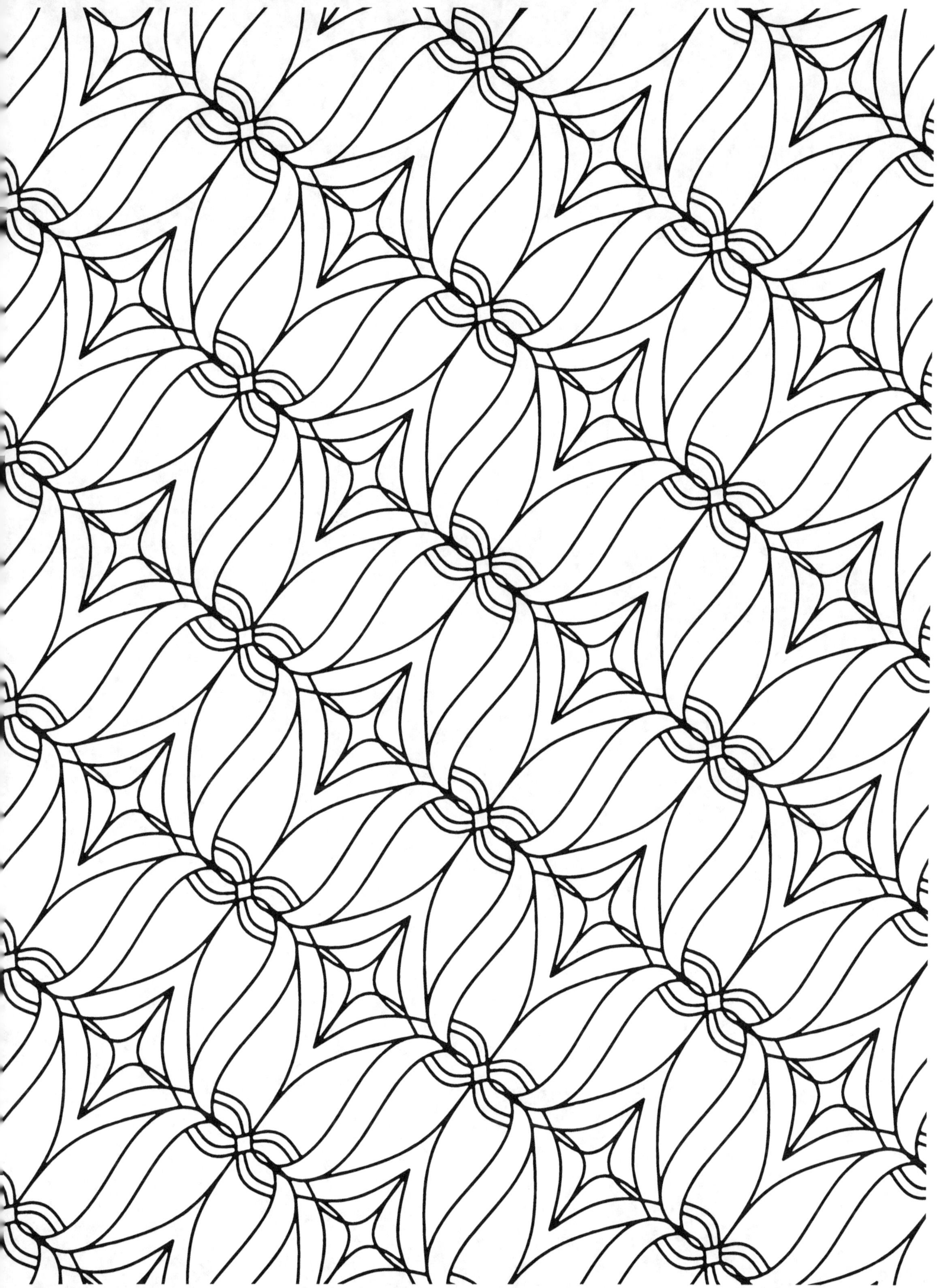

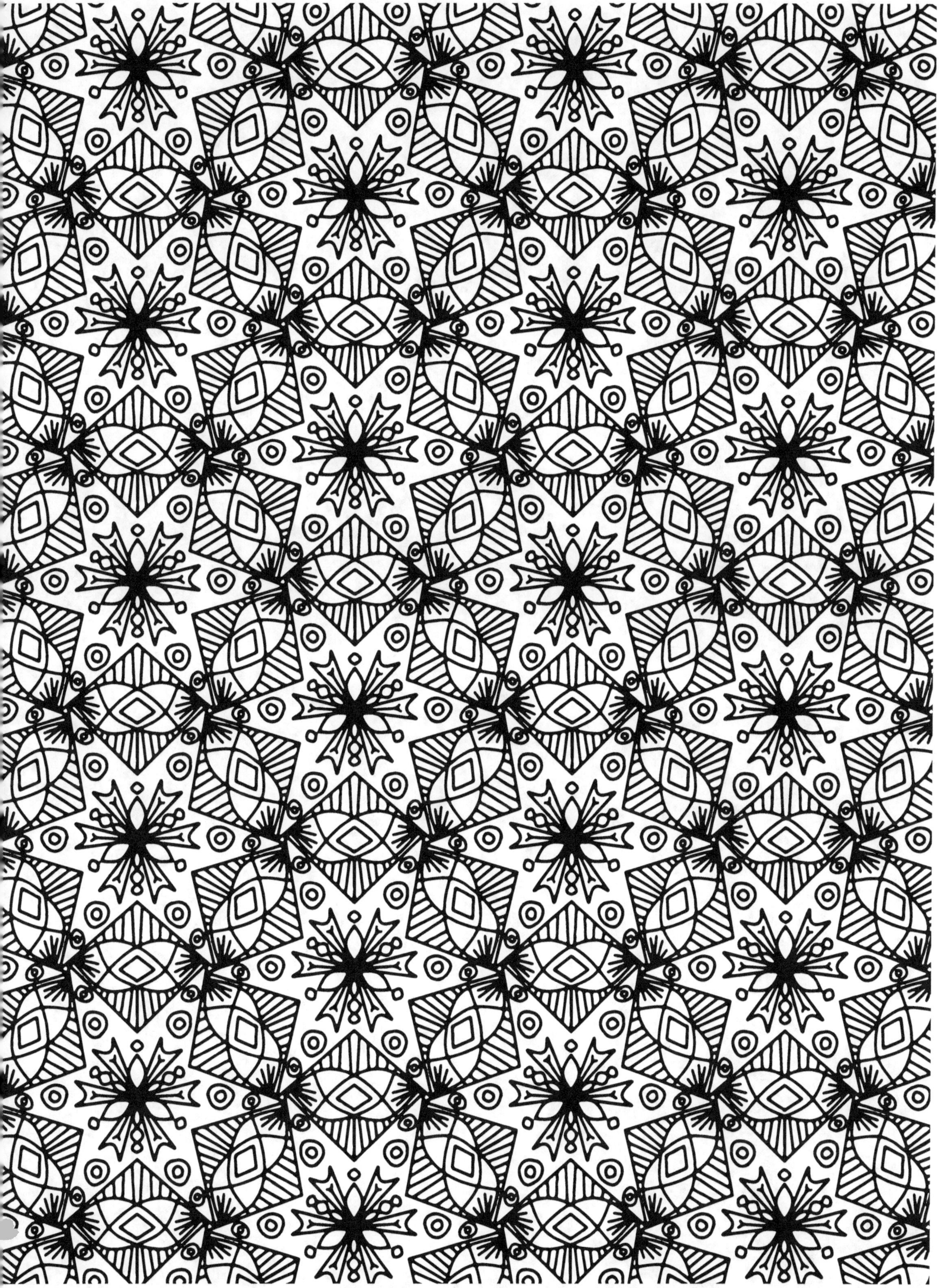

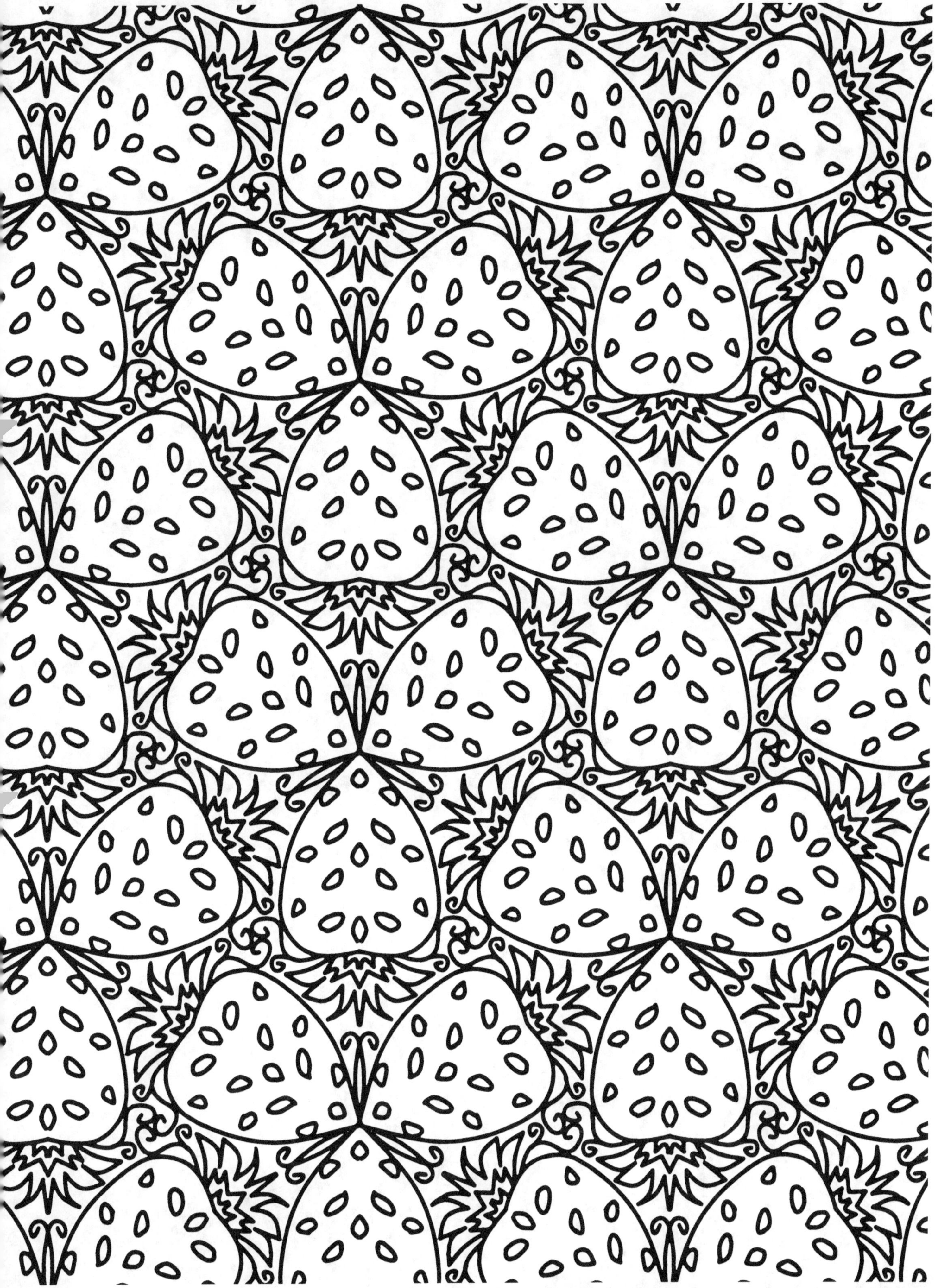

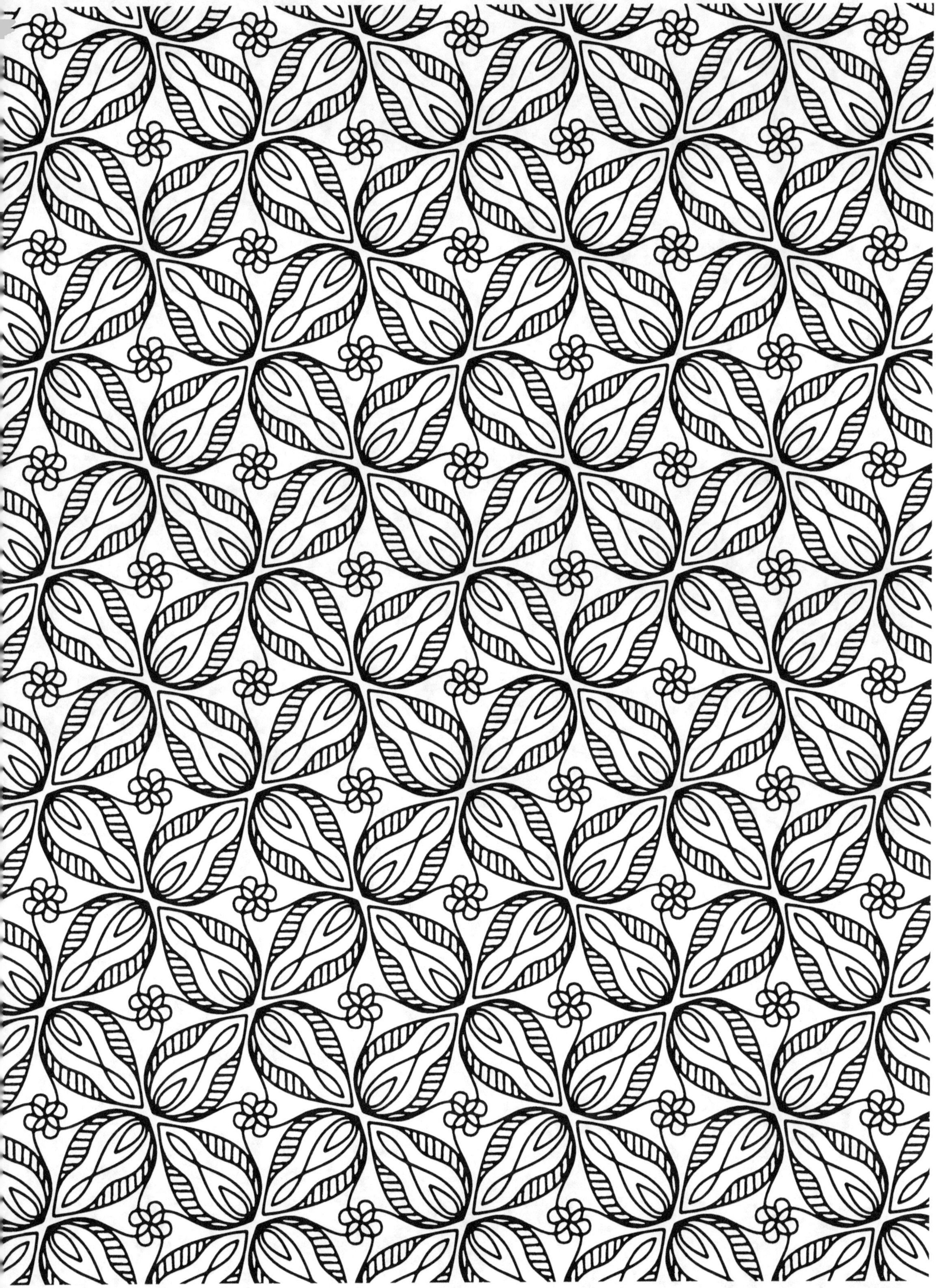

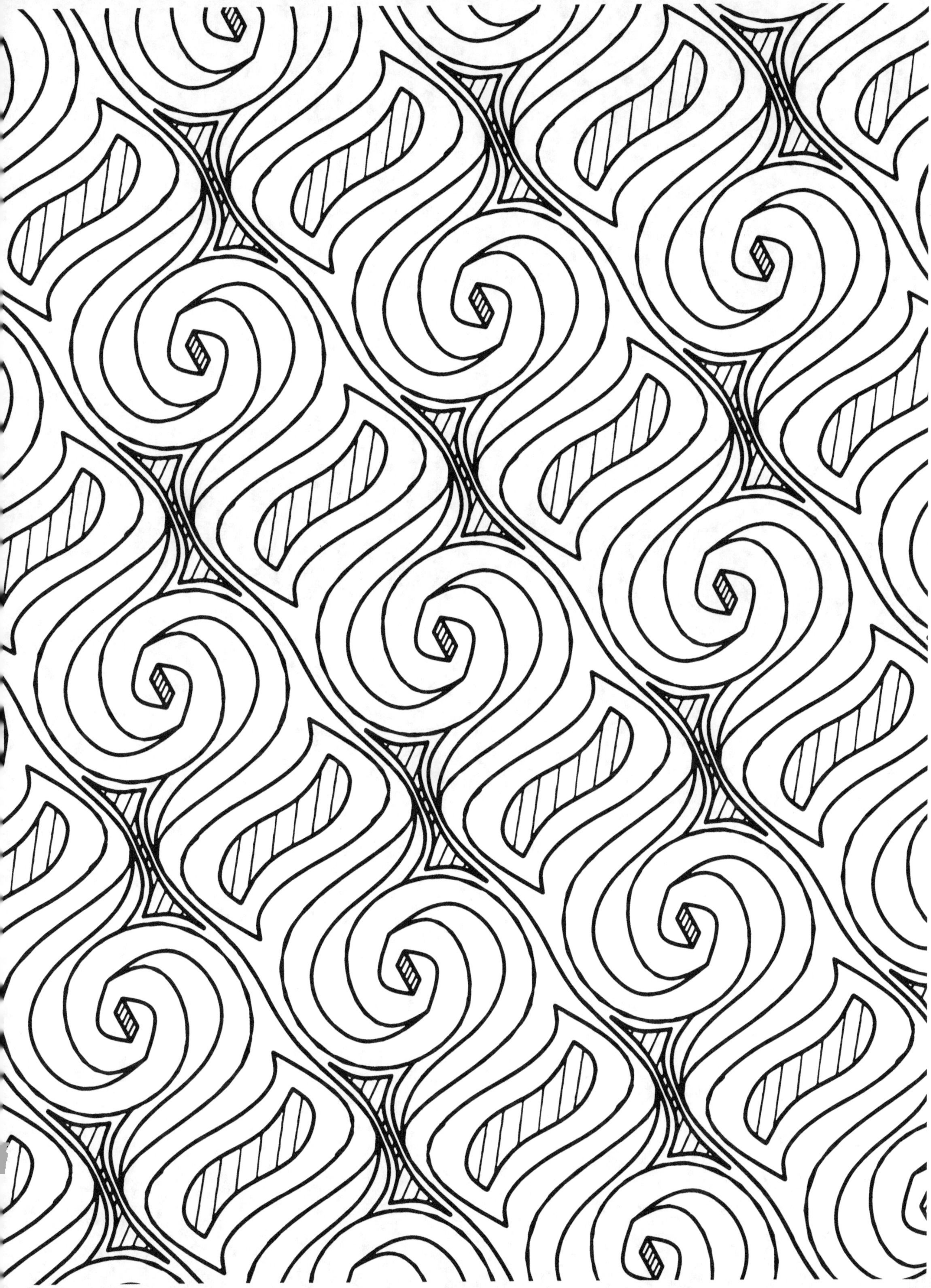

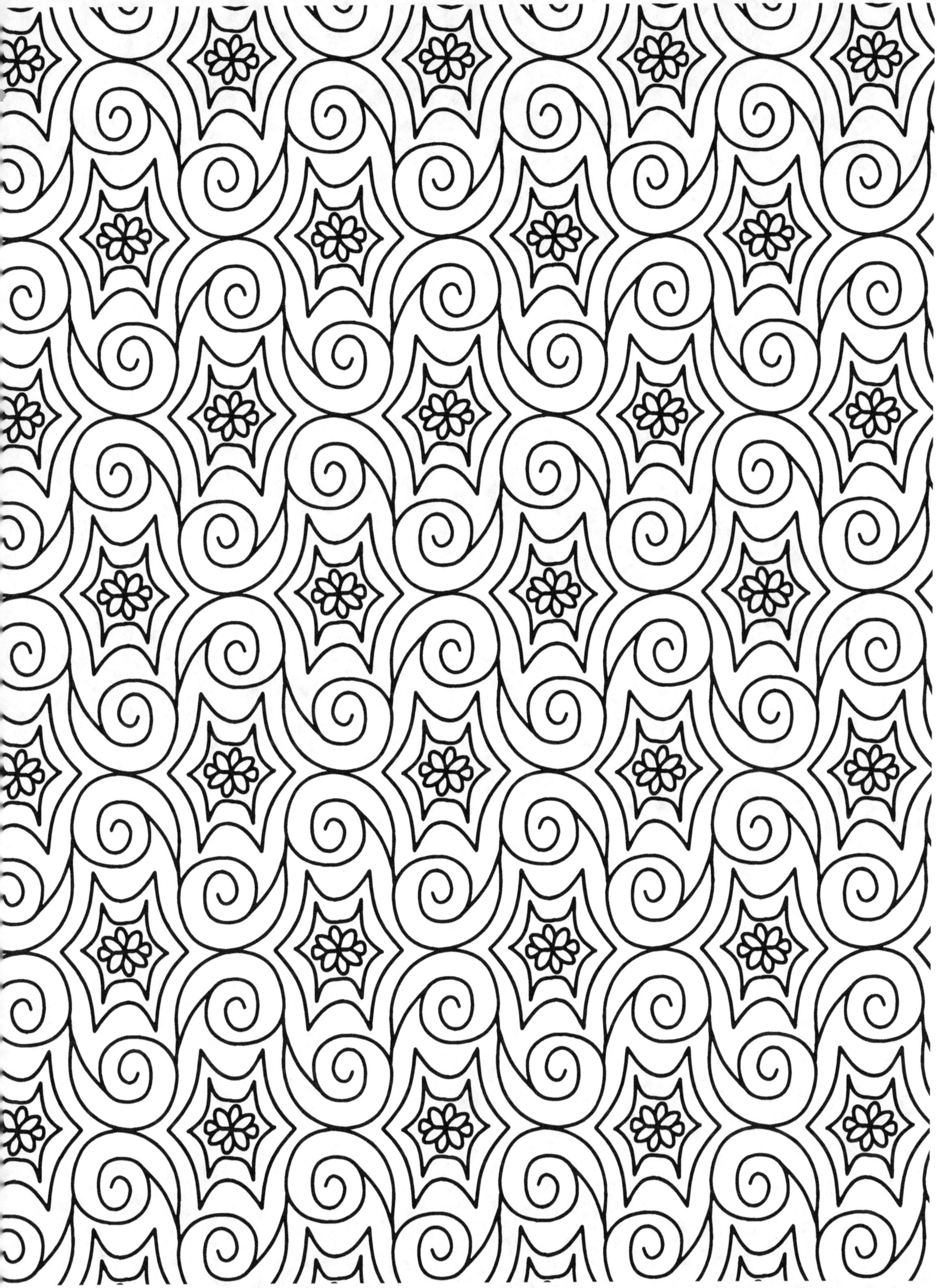

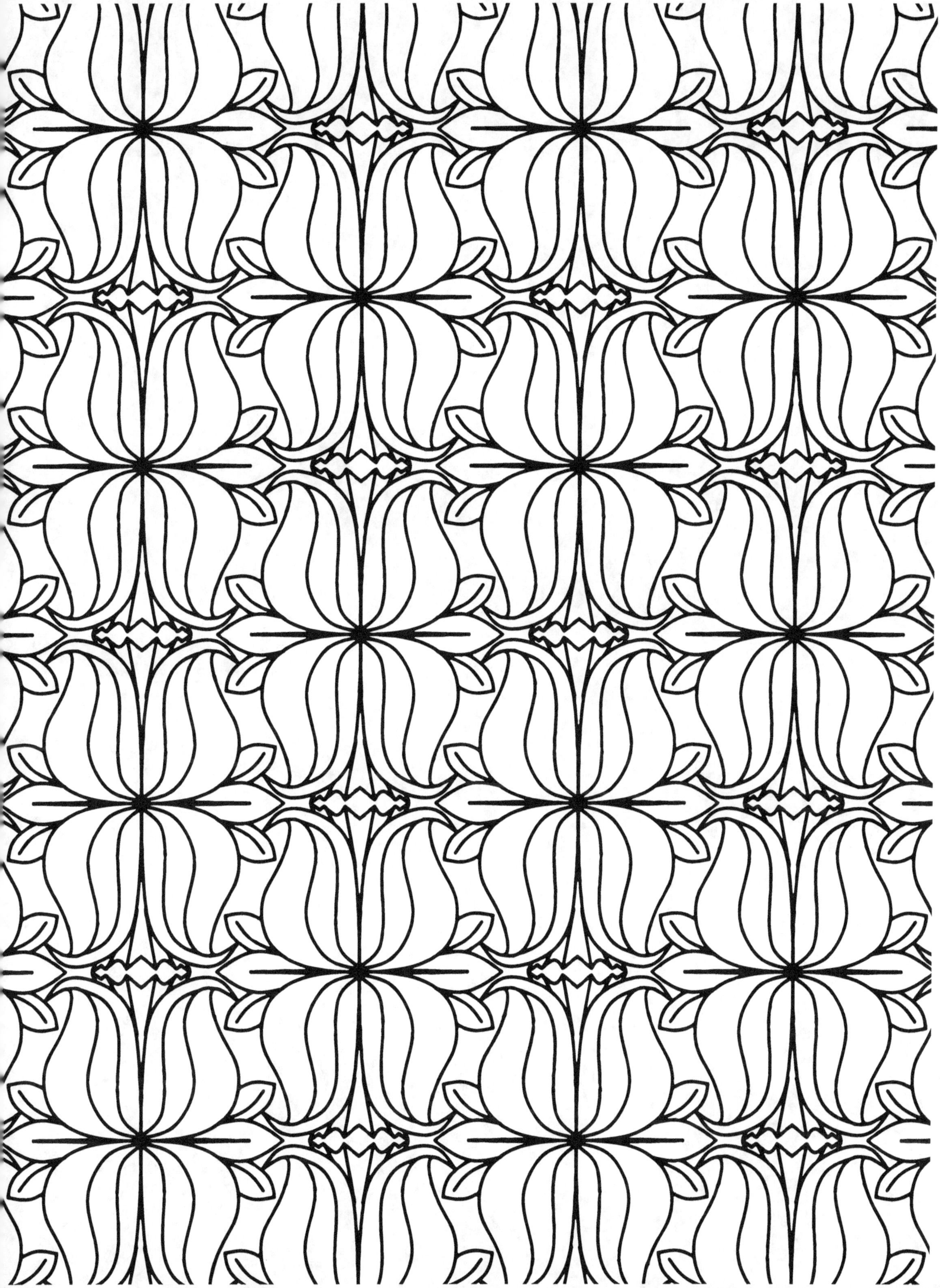

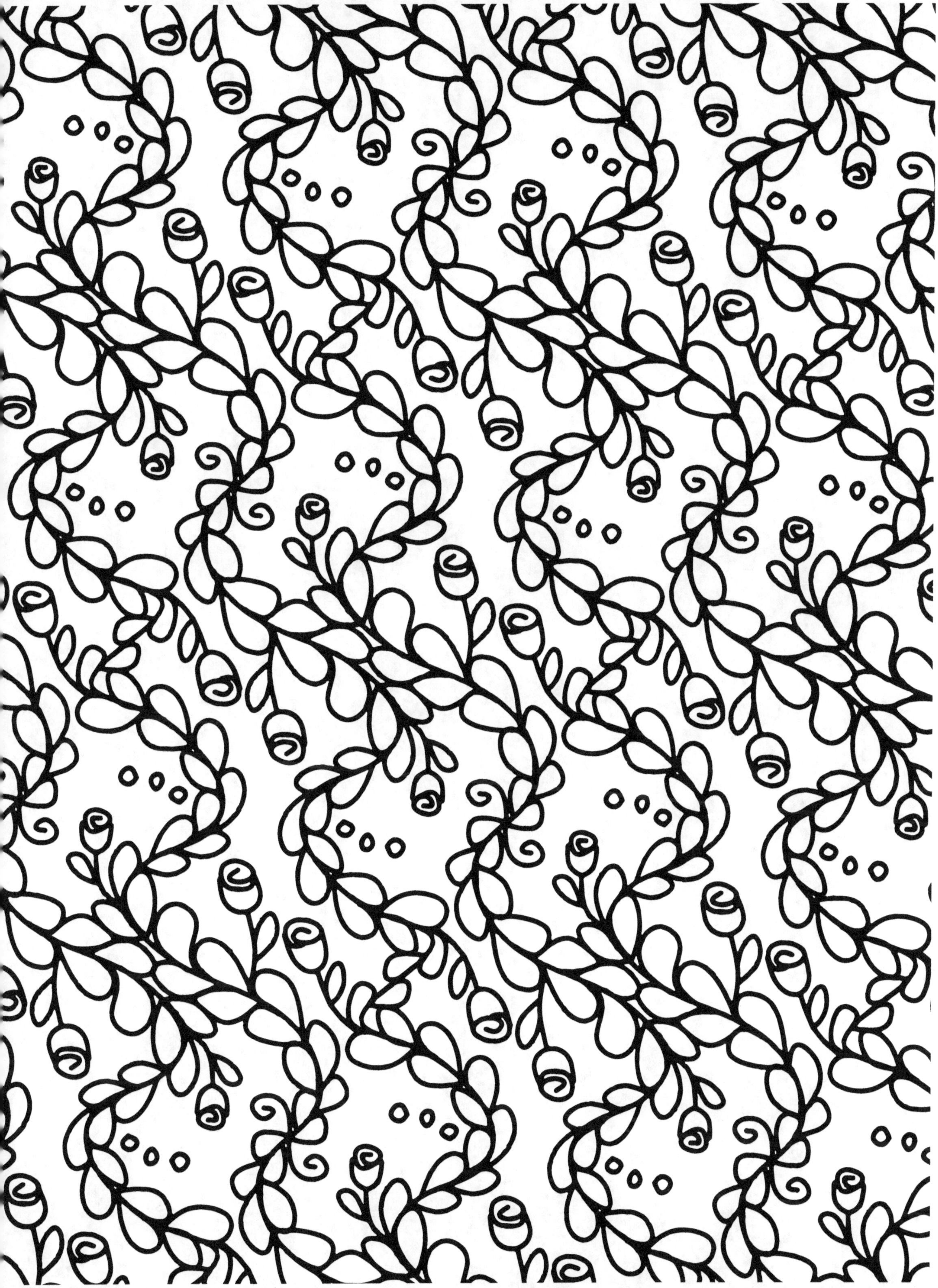

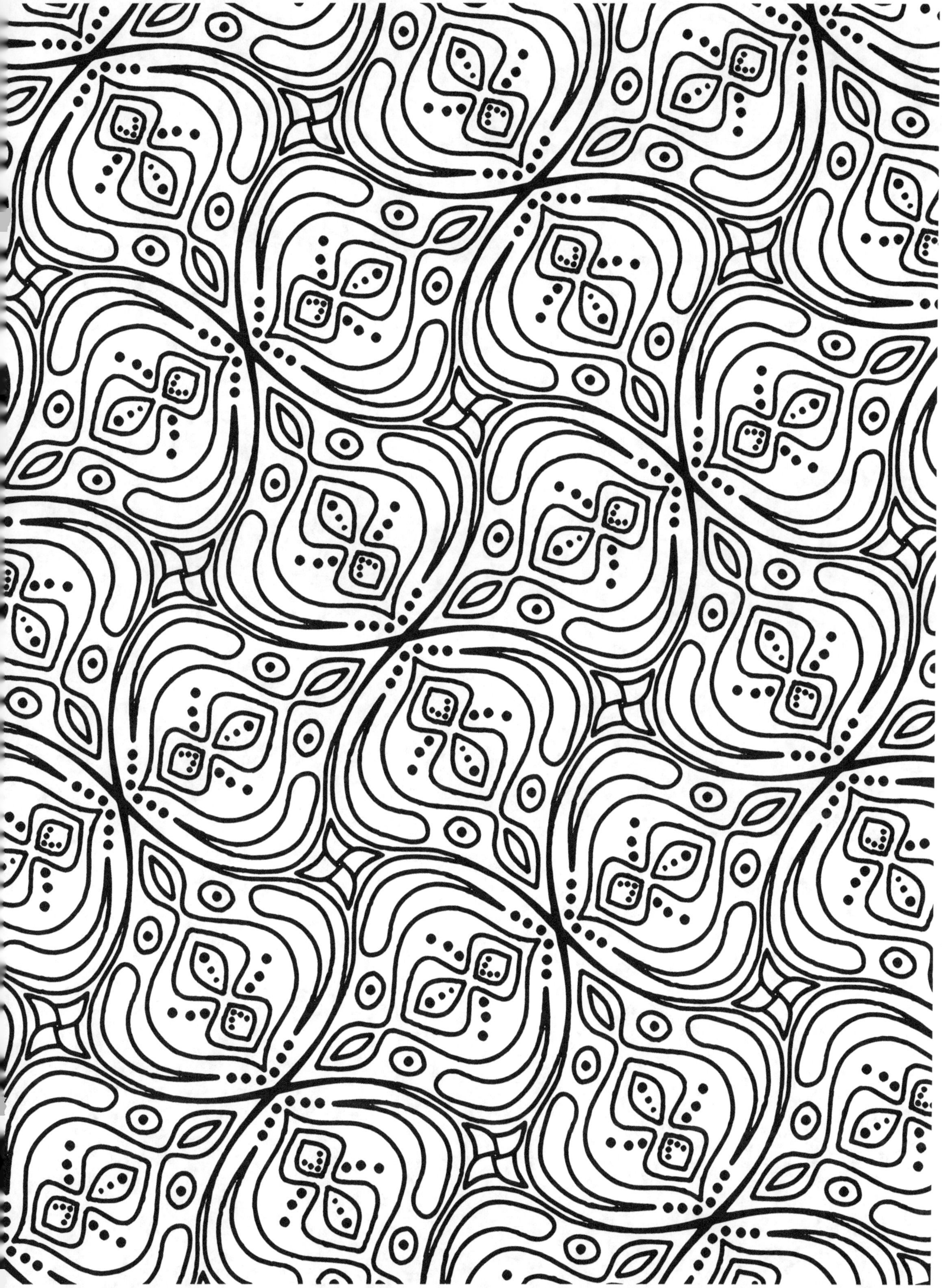

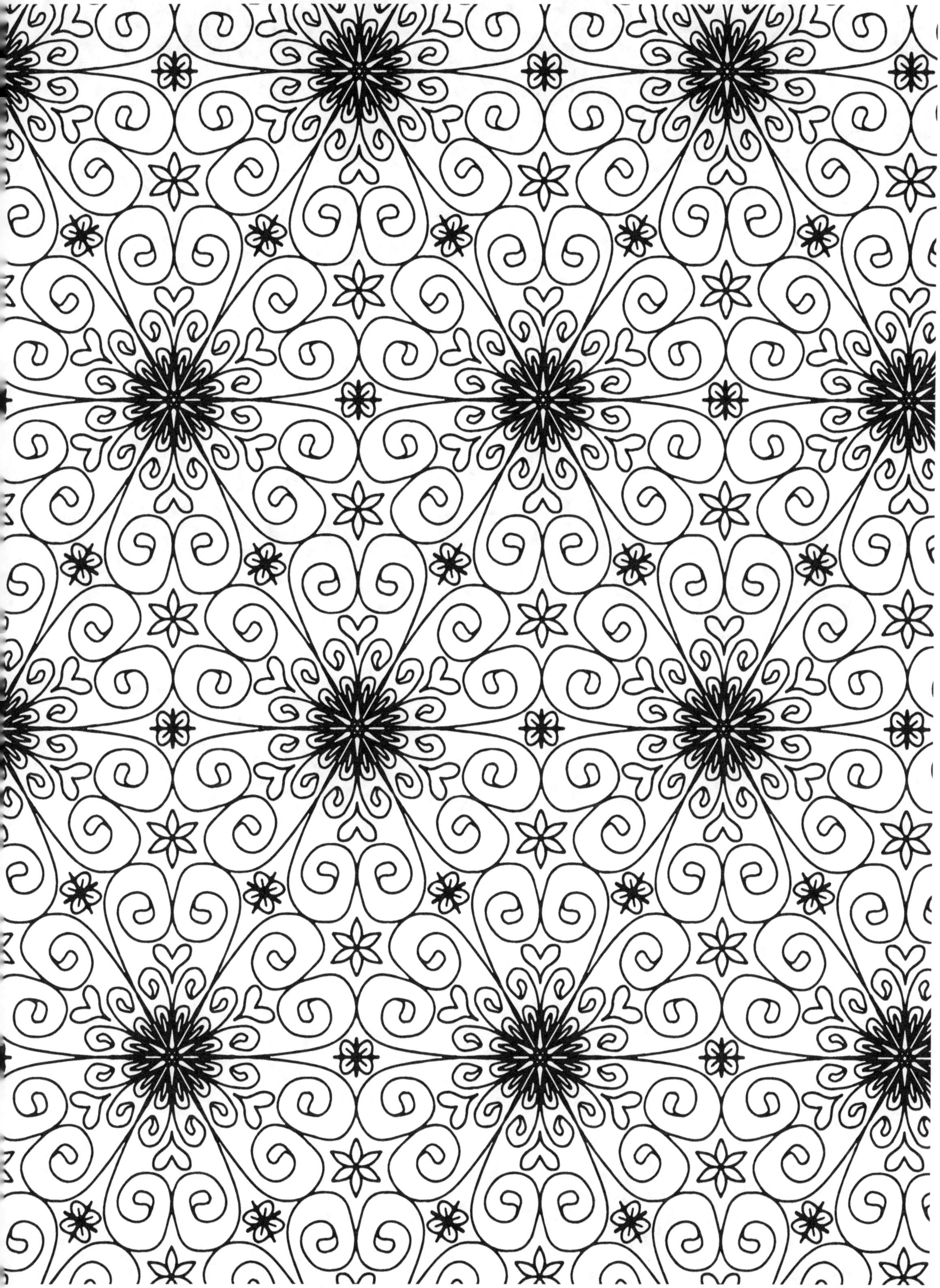

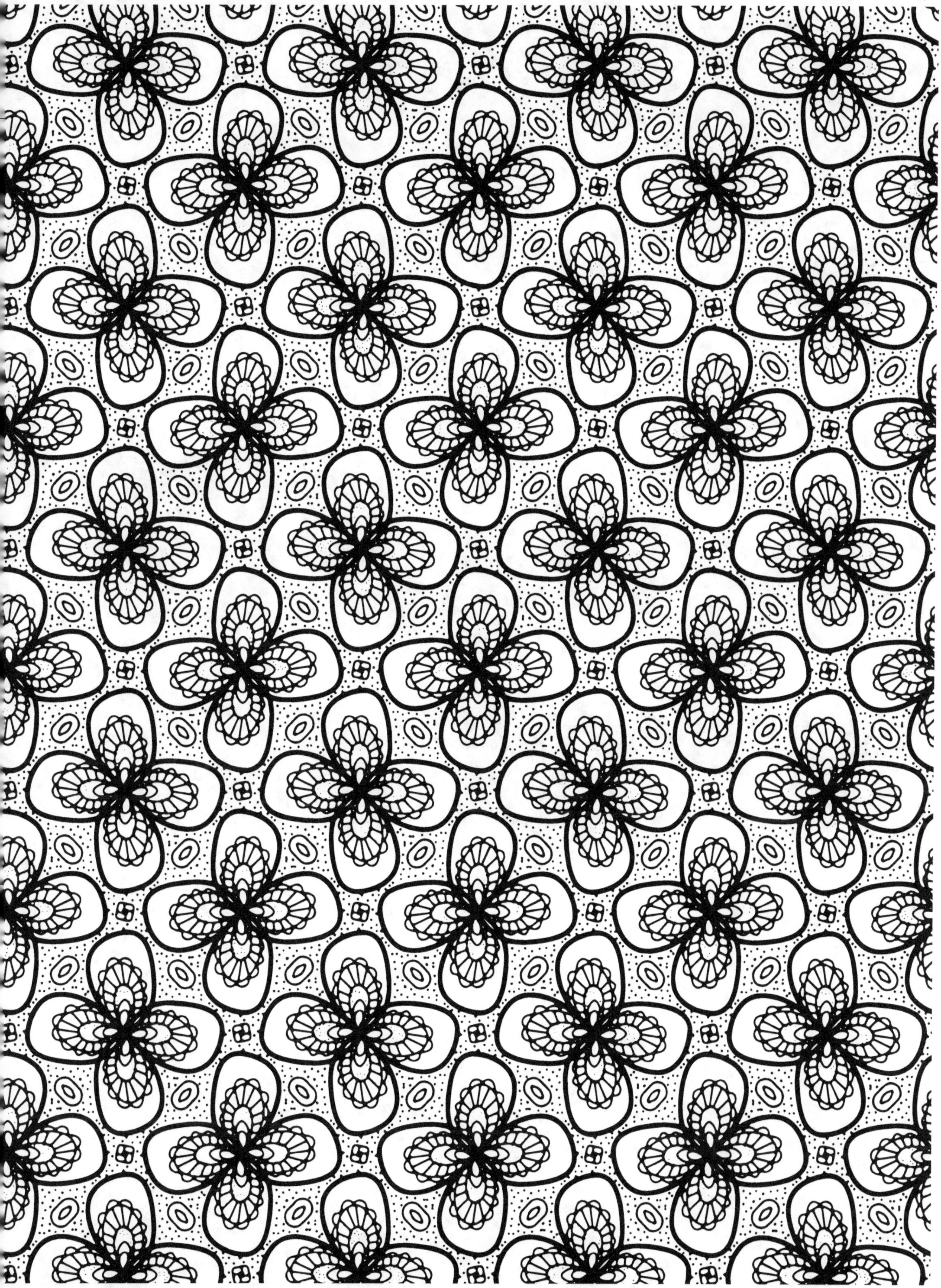

www.ingramcontent.com/pod-product-compliance
Lightning Source LLC
Chambersburg PA
CBHW081007170526
45158CB00010B/2953